Texas Real Estate License Exam: Best Test Prep Book to Help You Get Your License!

The Ultimate Workbook: Salesperson and Broker Exam-Passing Strategies

By: Blueocean Experts

Table of Content

Introduction

Welcome to "Texas Real Estate Learning: Texas Real Estate License Exam—Best Test Prep Book to Help You Get Your License!" If you're reading this, you're likely considering a career in one of the most dynamic, rewarding, and complex fields out there: real estate. And not just anywhere, but in the great state of Texas—a state as vast and diverse as the opportunities it offers in the property market. From the bustling metropolis of Houston to the cultural melting pot of Austin, from the historic charm of San Antonio to the ever-expanding suburbs of Dallas-Fort Worth, Texas is a state of endless real estate possibilities.

Why This Book?

The Texas Real Estate License Exam is your gateway to entering this fascinating world professionally. However, the exam is not to be taken lightly. It's a rigorous test of your knowledge on a wide range of topics, from property laws and contract types to ethics and agency relationships. This book aims to be your all-in-one guide to help you prepare for and pass the exam with flying colors. But we don't stop there. Beyond helping you clear the exam, this book is designed to give you a comprehensive understanding of the real estate business, particularly as it operates in the state of Texas.

What's Inside?

We've structured this book to be a step-by-step guide. It starts with an overview of the Texas real estate market, followed by a deep dive into the eligibility criteria and application process for the exam. We then move on to the exam format and the types of questions you can expect. Each subsequent chapter focuses on a specific topic that is covered in the exam, complete with mock questions and explanations to test your understanding of the subject matter.

Not Just for Beginners

While this book is an excellent resource for those new to real estate, it's also a valuable tool for seasoned professionals looking to brush up on current laws, trends, and best practices in the Texas real estate market. The real estate landscape is ever-changing, and even if you've been in the business for years, there's always something new to learn.

Your Journey Starts Here

Passing the Texas Real Estate License Exam is not just about memorizing facts; it's about understanding concepts, laws, and ethical standards that will govern your career. It's about laying a strong foundation upon which you can build a successful and ethical practice. This book aims to do just that—equip you with the knowledge and skills you'll need not just to pass the exam but to excel in your career.

- As you turn the pages of this book, you're not just preparing for an exam; you're taking a significant step in your professional journey. The real estate market in Texas is as diverse as it is large, offering a plethora of opportunities for those willing to put in the work. Whether you're looking to specialize in residential, commercial, or industrial properties, whether you're aiming to be a sales agent, a broker, or an investor, this book is your starting point.

Thank you for choosing this book as your guide. Let's embark on this journey together, toward a successful career in the Texas real estate market.

Understanding the Texas Real Estate Market

The Texas real estate market is as vast and varied as the state itself. From the sprawling metropolises of Houston and Dallas to the serene landscapes of the Hill Country, Texas offers a range of opportunities for real estate professionals. This chapter aims to provide a comprehensive understanding of the market, including key sectors, growth drivers, and challenges. Whether you're a newcomer to the field or a seasoned professional, understanding the nuances of the Texas real estate market is crucial for your success.

The Texas Economy: A Brief Overview

Before diving into the real estate specifics, it's essential to understand the broader economic context in which the market operates. Texas has a diverse economy, with significant contributions from the energy sector, technology, healthcare, and more. The state's GDP ranks among the highest in the nation, making it a hub for both residential and commercial real estate activities.

Residential Real Estate

Urban Markets

The residential sector in cities like Houston, Dallas, Austin, and San Antonio has seen consistent growth over the years. These cities offer a mix of housing options, from high-rise condos to suburban single-family homes.

- Market Trends

Houston: Known for its energy sector, the city has a diverse housing market with a focus on affordability.

Dallas: A hub for tech and finance, Dallas has seen a surge in luxury apartments and condos.

Austin: With a booming tech industry, Austin has a high demand for residential spaces close to tech parks.

San Antonio: Tourism and military bases drive the housing demand, with a focus on family-friendly neighborhoods.

- Rural Markets

Rural Texas offers different opportunities, with large plots of land and ranch-style homes being the norm. Areas like the Hill Country are popular for vacation homes and retirement communities.

- Market Trends

Land value: Generally lower than urban areas but has been appreciating due to increased interest in rural living.

Types of Properties: Farmhouses, ranches, and large estates are common.

Commercial Real Estate

- Office Spaces

Texas is home to numerous Fortune 500 companies, creating a robust market for office spaces, particularly in cities like Houston and Dallas.

- Market Trends

Co-working Spaces: With the rise of startups, co-working spaces have become increasingly popular.

Green Buildings: There's a growing trend towards sustainable construction.

- Retail and Industrial Spaces

The retail market is thriving due to Texas' strong economy and growing population. Industrial real estate, particularly near ports and transportation hubs, is also a significant sector.

- Market Trends

E-commerce Impact: The rise of online shopping has led to an increase in demand for warehouse spaces.

Mixed-Use Developments: Combining retail, office, and residential spaces in one development is becoming more common.

Challenges and Risks

Regulatory Hurdles: Texas has its own set of real estate laws and regulations that professionals must navigate.

Market Saturation: In some sectors, particularly in urban residential areas, there's a risk of oversupply.

Economic Fluctuations: The Texas real estate market isn't immune to broader economic trends, including recessions and booms.

Conclusion

Understanding the Texas real estate market is crucial for anyone looking to succeed in this field. The market is diverse, offering a range of opportunities across different sectors and regions. However, it also comes with its own set of challenges that professionals must navigate skillfully. This chapter aims to provide you with the foundational knowledge required to understand and succeed in the Texas real estate market.

Eligibility Criteria

Becoming a licensed real estate agent in Texas is a multi-step process that begins with meeting specific eligibility criteria. This chapter aims to provide a comprehensive guide to the qualifications and requirements you must fulfill to sit for the Texas Real Estate License Exam. Understanding these criteria is crucial for planning your career path and ensuring you're well-prepared for the licensing process.

Age Requirements

In Texas, you must be at least 18 years old to apply for a real estate license. This age requirement is non-negotiable and applies to all applicants, regardless of their educational or professional background.

Educational Requirements

- High School Diploma or Equivalent

A high school diploma or its equivalent, such as a GED, is a basic requirement for becoming a real estate agent in Texas.

- Pre-Licensing Education

Before you can take the Texas Real Estate License Exam, you must complete 180 classroom hours of qualifying real estate courses. These courses are divided into six 30-hour subjects:

Principles of Real Estate I & II: These courses cover the basics of property law, contracts, and finance.

Law of Agency: This course delves into the legal aspects of real estate representation.

Law of Contracts: This focuses on the legal requirements for real estate contracts in Texas.

Promulgated Contract Forms: This course covers the standardized forms used in Texas real estate transactions.

Real Estate Finance: This course provides an overview of mortgage processes and other financial aspects of real estate.

Residency and Citizenship

Texas does not require you to be a resident of the state to become a licensed real estate agent. However, you must be a U.S. citizen or a lawfully admitted alien.

Background Check and Fingerprints

All applicants must undergo a background check and submit fingerprints to the Texas Department of Public Safety. A criminal history does not automatically disqualify you, but certain offenses may require you to provide additional documentation or undergo a formal review process.

Application Process

Submit an Application: The first step is to submit an application to the Texas Real Estate Commission (TREC).

Pay Fees: There is an application fee that varies depending on the type of license you're applying for.

Submit Educational Transcripts: You must provide proof of completed educational requirements.

Background Check: After submitting your application, you'll receive instructions for the background check and fingerprinting.

Exam Eligibility: Once your application is approved, you'll receive a notification of your eligibility to sit for the exam.

Exam Requirements

Exam Format

The Texas Real Estate License Exam consists of two parts: the national portion and the state-specific portion. You must pass both to obtain your license.

Exam Fees

There is a separate fee for the exam, which you must pay when scheduling your test date.

Passing Score

You must achieve a passing score on both portions of the exam to be eligible for a license. If you fail one part, you can retake it without having to retake the part you passed.

Post-Exam Requirements

After passing the exam, you must:

Activate Your License: You'll need to pay an activation fee to TREC.

Sponsorship: To practice as a real estate agent, you must be sponsored by a licensed Texas real estate broker.

Continuing Education: Texas requires ongoing education to maintain your license, including 18 hours of Continuing Education every two years.

Conclusion

Understanding the eligibility criteria for the Texas Real Estate License Exam is the first step in your journey to becoming a licensed real estate agent in the state. This chapter has provided a comprehensive overview of the qualifications and requirements you must meet, from educational prerequisites to post-exam procedures. By familiarizing yourself with these criteria, you can better plan your career path and ensure you're well-prepared for each stage of the licensing process.

Application Process

The application process for obtaining a real estate license in Texas is a multi-step journey that requires careful planning, attention to detail, and adherence to specific guidelines set forth by the Texas Real Estate Commission (TREC). This chapter aims to provide a comprehensive guide to navigating this process, from initial preparations to post-submission steps.

Pre-Application Preparations

Before you even begin the application process, there are several preparatory steps you must complete:

Educational Requirements

As mentioned in the previous chapter, you must complete 180 hours of pre-licensing education. Make sure to obtain certificates or transcripts as proof of completion.

Background Check and Fingerprints

You'll need to undergo a background check and fingerprinting through the Texas Department of Public Safety. This should be done before applying to ensure that there are no issues that could delay your application.

Financial Planning

There are various fees associated with the application process, including the application fee, exam fee, and potential costs for fingerprinting and background checks. Budget accordingly.

The Application Form

- Where to Find It

The application form can be found on the TREC website. It's crucial to download the most recent version to ensure you're filling out the correct information.

- Sections of the Application

Personal Information: This includes your full name, address, and contact details.

Eligibility Criteria: Here, you'll confirm that you meet all the eligibility criteria discussed in the previous chapter.

Educational Background: You'll need to list the courses you've completed, along with the names of the institutions and dates of completion.

Criminal History: If applicable, you'll need to provide details about any criminal history.

Employment History: Some applications may require a brief employment history, especially if you've worked in related fields.

References: Some forms may require professional references.

- Tips for Filling Out the Application

Be Honest: All the information you provide must be accurate and truthful.

Be Thorough: Incomplete applications can result in delays or denials.

Check for Errors: Double-check all entries for mistakes before submitting.

Submission Process

Online vs. Mail

You can submit your application either online through the TREC website or by mailing a paper application. Online is faster but ensure you have digital copies of all required documents.

Required Documents

Along with your application form, you'll need to submit:

- *Proof of completed educational requirements*
- *Background check and fingerprinting results*
- *Payment for the application fee*

Payment Methods

Online applications usually accept credit or debit cards, while mailed applications may require a check or money order.

After Submission

Application Review

Once TREC receives your application, it will undergo a review process that can take several weeks. You'll receive a notification once your application is approved or if additional information is needed.

Exam Eligibility

After approval, you'll receive an eligibility letter that allows you to schedule your exam.

License Activation

Upon passing the exam, you'll need to activate your license by paying an activation fee and obtaining sponsorship from a licensed Texas real estate broker.

Common Pitfalls and How to Avoid Them

Missing Documents: Ensure all required documents are submitted to avoid delays.

Incorrect Information: Double-check all entries to avoid the need for corrections, which can also cause delays.

Failure to Update Information: If any information changes after submission (e.g., address), update it promptly with TREC.

Conclusion

The application process for obtaining a Texas real estate license may seem daunting, but with careful planning and attention to detail, it can be navigated smoothly. This chapter has provided a step-by-step guide to help you understand what to expect and how to prepare. By following these guidelines, you'll be well on your way to becoming a licensed real estate agent in Texas.

Exam Format

Understanding the format of the Texas Real Estate License Exam is crucial for effective preparation and ultimately, for passing the test. This chapter will provide an in-depth look at the exam's structure, types of questions you'll encounter, and strategies for tackling each section.

Overview of the Exam

The Texas Real Estate License Exam is administered by Pearson VUE and consists of two main sections:

National Portion: This section tests your understanding of general real estate principles and practices that apply across the United States.

State Portion: This section focuses on real estate laws, regulations, and practices specific to Texas.

- Time Allocation

National Portion: 150 minutes
State Portion: 90 minutes

- Number of Questions

National Portion: 85 questions
State Portion: 40 questions

- Passing Score

National Portion: 70%
State Portion: 70%

Types of Questions

Multiple-Choice Questions

The exam is entirely multiple-choice, with four answer options for each question. The questions are designed to test your knowledge, comprehension, application, and analysis skills.

Scenario-Based Questions

Some questions may present a short scenario or case study, followed by one or more questions related to the scenario.

National Portion

- Topics Covered

Property Ownership and Land Use Controls: This includes questions on types of ownership, property rights, and land use regulations.

Laws of Agency and Fiduciary Duties: This covers the legal aspects of the agent-client relationship.

Property Valuation and Financial Analysis: This includes questions on appraisal methods and investment analysis.

- Strategies for the National Portion

Time Management: Allocate around 1.5 minutes per question.

Elimination Method: Use the process of elimination to narrow down choices.

Flagging: Flag questions you're unsure about and revisit them if time permits.

State Portion

- Topics Covered

Texas Real Estate Commission (TREC) Rules and Regulations: This includes questions on licensing requirements and disciplinary actions.

Texas Real Estate Laws: This covers property laws, contract laws, and agency laws specific to Texas.

Special Topics: This includes questions on property management, leasing, and other specialized areas.

- Strategies for the State Portion

Focus on Texas-Specific Laws: The state portion will test your knowledge on laws and regulations unique to Texas, so focus your study efforts accordingly.

Review Past Exams: While the questions won't be the same, reviewing past exams can give you a sense of the types of questions you'll encounter.

General Exam Tips

Read Carefully: Misreading a question can lead to an incorrect answer.

Pace Yourself: Keep an eye on the clock to ensure you have enough time to answer all questions.

Stay Calm: Anxiety can affect performance, so take deep breaths if you start to feel overwhelmed.

What to Bring to the Exam

Two Forms of Identification: One must be a government-issued photo ID.

Confirmation Number: This is provided when you schedule your exam.

Calculator: Basic, non-programmable calculators are usually allowed.

Conclusion

Understanding the format of the Texas Real Estate License Exam is a critical step in your preparation. This chapter has provided a comprehensive overview of what to expect and how to prepare for both the National and State portions of the exam. With this knowledge in hand, you can tailor your study plan to focus on the areas that will be most crucial for passing the exam.

Property Ownership and Land Use Controls

Understanding the intricacies of property ownership and land use controls is vital for anyone involved in the real estate industry. This chapter aims to offer a comprehensive, in-depth look at the various forms of property ownership, zoning laws, environmental regulations, and other land use controls that have a direct impact on the real estate market.

Types of Property Ownership

- Fee Simple Absolute

Fee simple absolute is the most complete form of ownership. The owner has the right to control, use, and transfer the property without any restrictions. However, it's essential to note that even fee simple ownership is subject to public and private limitations such as zoning laws, easements, and covenants.

- Advantages and Disadvantages

The primary advantage of fee simple absolute is the high degree of control it offers. However, the downside is that the owner is responsible for all taxes and maintenance.

- Life Estate

A life estate is a unique form of ownership where the owner, known as the life tenant, has the right to use and possess the property for the duration of their life. Upon their death, the property reverts to a designated person, known as the remainderman.

Legal Implications - Life estates can be complex when it comes to legal rights and responsibilities. The life tenant cannot make significant changes to the property that would affect its value for the remainderman.

- Leasehold Estate

In a leasehold estate, the tenant has the right to occupy and use the property for a fixed period, usually defined in a lease agreement. The landlord retains the ownership of the property.

Types of Leasehold Estates

Fixed-Term: Ends on a specific date.
Periodic: Renews automatically until terminated.
At-Will: Can be terminated at any time.

- Joint Tenancy and Tenancy in Common

Joint tenancy and tenancy in common are forms of co-ownership. While joint tenants own equal shares and have survivorship rights, tenants in common may own unequal shares and can transfer their shares independently.

Legal Procedures - Both forms of co-ownership have specific legal procedures for transfer and sale, often requiring the consent of the other owners.

Zoning Laws

Zoning laws are public regulations that control land use. They are enacted by local governments and can vary widely from one jurisdiction to another.

- Residential Zoning

Residential zoning laws dictate the types of structures that can be built in certain areas. These laws often specify density limits, parking requirements, and even architectural styles.

Case Studies:

Single-Family Zones: Often restrict the property to one dwelling unit.
Multi-Family Zones: Allow for apartments and condominiums.

- Commercial and Industrial Zoning

Commercial and industrial zoning laws are designed to segregate businesses from residential areas. These laws often specify types of businesses, parking requirements, and even operating hours.

Zoning Appeals - It's possible to appeal a zoning decision, but the process can be lengthy and expensive.

Environmental Regulations

Environmental laws aim to protect natural resources and public health. They can significantly impact land use and property development.

- Wetlands and Endangered Species

Both federal and state laws often protect wetlands and endangered species. Any development in these areas usually requires a permit and may be subject to restrictions.

Legal Cases - Several landmark cases have set precedents for environmental regulations affecting property use, such as the Clean Water Act and the Endangered Species Act.

- Pollution Control

Various laws regulate air and water pollution, waste disposal, and chemical storage. Failure to comply can result in hefty fines and legal action.

EPA Guidelines - The Environmental Protection Agency (EPA) provides guidelines and standards that property owners must follow.

Eminent Domain and Restrictive Covenants

- Eminent Domain

Eminent domain is the power of the government to take private property for public use. The owner must be compensated at fair market value.

Legal Challenges - Legal challenges to eminent domain often focus on what constitutes "public use" and "fair compensation."

- Restrictive Covenants and HOAs

Restrictive covenants are private agreements that restrict the use of land. Homeowners Associations (HOAs) often enforce these covenants.

HOA Rules - HOAs can have a significant impact on property use, from exterior paint colors to types of fencing allowed.

Conclusion

Understanding property ownership and land use controls is not just beneficial but crucial for anyone involved in the real estate industry. These laws and regulations shape how property can be used, valued, and transferred, affecting everyone from individual homeowners to large-scale developers and real estate professionals.

Mock Exam Property Ownership and Land Use Controls

➡1. What is the most complete form of property ownership?

A. Life Estate

B. Leasehold Estate

C. Fee Simple Absolute

D. Joint Tenancy

Answer: C

Fee Simple Absolute provides the most complete form of ownership, giving the owner the right to control, use, and transfer the property without any restrictions.

➡2. What is the primary disadvantage of Fee Simple Absolute?

A. Limited control

B. No right to transfer

C. Responsibility for taxes and maintenance

D. No survivorship rights

Answer: C

The owner is responsible for all taxes and maintenance, which is the primary disadvantage of Fee Simple Absolute.

➡3. Who is the designated person to whom property reverts in a Life Estate?

A. Life Tenant

B. Remainderman

C. Joint Tenant

D. Leaseholder

Answer: B

The property reverts to a designated person known as the "remainderman" in a Life Estate.

➡4. What is the right to occupy and use property for a fixed period called?

    A. Fee Simple

    B. Life Estate

    C. Leasehold Estate

    D. Tenancy in Common

Answer: C

A Leasehold Estate gives the tenant the right to occupy and use the property for a fixed period.

➡5. What type of co-ownership allows for unequal shares?

    A. Joint Tenancy

    B. Tenancy in Common

    C. Leasehold Estate

    D. Life Estate

Answer: B

Tenancy in Common allows for unequal shares and independent transfer of shares.

➡6. What are zoning laws primarily designed to do?

    A. Increase property value

    B. Control land use

    C. Encourage co-ownership

    D. Protect endangered species

Answer: B

Zoning laws are public regulations enacted by local governments to control land use.

➡7. What type of zoning law often restricts a property to one dwelling unit?

  A. Commercial

  B. Multi-Family

  C. Single-Family

  D. Industrial

Answer: C

Single-Family Zones often restrict the property to one dwelling unit.

➡8. What is the power of the government to take private property for public use called?

  A. Restrictive Covenant

  B. Eminent Domain

  C. Zoning

  D. Environmental Regulation

Answer: B

Eminent Domain is the power of the government to take private property for public use.

➡9. What type of private agreement restricts the use of land?

  A. Zoning Law

  B. Eminent Domain

  C. Restrictive Covenant

  D. Lease Agreement

Answer: C

Restrictive Covenants are private agreements that restrict the use of land.

➡10. What agency provides guidelines for environmental regulations affecting property use?

    A. HUD

    B. EPA

    C. HOA

    D. IRS

Answer: B

The Environmental Protection Agency (EPA) provides guidelines and standards that property owners must follow.

➡11. What is the primary purpose of a building permit?

    A. To increase property taxes

    B. To ensure construction meets local codes

    C. To limit the number of buildings in an area

    D. To designate historical landmarks

Answer: B

A building permit ensures that construction meets local building codes and regulations.

➡12. What is a variance in the context of zoning laws?

    A. A change in property taxes

    B. An exception to zoning rules

    C. A type of building permit

    D. A form of restrictive covenant

Answer: B

A variance is an exception to zoning rules, usually granted by a local government.

➟13. What is the primary purpose of a deed restriction?

    A. To limit property taxes

    B. To control land use

    C. To designate ownership

    D. To establish a lease agreement

Answer: B

A deed restriction is used to control how the land is used and often runs with the land, affecting future owners.

➟14. What is the difference between a general lien and a specific lien?

    A. General lien is voluntary; specific lien is involuntary

    B. General lien affects all properties; specific lien affects one property

    C. General lien has no time limit; specific lien expires

    D. General lien is imposed by the government; specific lien is private

Answer: B

A general lien affects all properties owned by an individual, whereas a specific lien affects only one property.

➟15. What is the primary purpose of the Fair Housing Act?

    A. To limit property taxes

    B. To prevent discrimination in housing

    C. To control land use

    D. To establish zoning laws

Answer: B

The Fair Housing Act aims to prevent discrimination based on race, color, religion, sex, or national origin in housing.

➡ **16. What is the doctrine of "prior appropriation"?**

    A. First come, first served for water rights

    B. Equal distribution of natural resources

    C. Government's right to control land use

    D. The oldest building has historical status

Answer: A

The doctrine of "prior appropriation" is often used in Western states to allocate water rights based on a first-come, first-served basis.

➡ **17. What is the Homestead Exemption primarily designed to do?**

    A. Protect a portion of home value from creditors

    B. Reduce property taxes

    C. Encourage home ownership

    D. Protect against eminent domain

Answer: A

The Homestead Exemption is designed to protect a portion of the home's value from creditors.

➡ **18. What is "adverse possession"?**

    A. Illegal occupation of a property

    B. Acquiring property rights through extended, open, and hostile possession

    C. A form of eminent domain

    D. A type of zoning violation

Answer: B

Adverse possession allows an individual to acquire property rights through extended, open, and hostile possession of the property.

➡ 19. What is the primary purpose of a "buffer zone" in zoning?

    A. To separate residential and commercial areas

    B. To protect natural resources

    C. To designate historical landmarks

    D. To increase property value

Answer: A

A "buffer zone" is often used to separate different types of land uses, such as residential and commercial areas.

➡ 20. What is "inclusionary zoning"?

    A. Zoning that includes multiple land uses

    B. Zoning that requires a percentage of affordable housing

    C. Zoning that excludes certain types of buildings

    D. Zoning that includes environmental protections

Answer: B

Inclusionary zoning requires developers to include a certain percentage of affordable housing in new developments.

➡ 21. What is a "master plan" in the context of urban development?

    A. A detailed layout of a single building

    B. A long-term planning document

    C. A short-term budget plan

    D. A list of approved contractors

Answer: B

A master plan is a long-term planning document that provides a conceptual layout to guide future growth and development.

➡ 22. What is "downzoning"?

A. Increasing the density allowed in an area
B. Decreasing the density allowed in an area
C. Changing commercial zones to residential
D. Changing residential zones to commercial

Answer: B

Downzoning is the act of rezoning land to decrease the density of allowable development, often from commercial to residential.

➡ 23. What is the primary purpose of "impact fees"?

A. To fund public services like schools and roads
B. To increase property taxes
C. To discourage development
D. To fund private construction projects

Answer: A

Impact fees are charges on new development to pay for the construction or expansion of off-site capital improvements like roads and schools.

➡ 24. What is "spot zoning"?

A. Zoning based on geographic features
B. Rezoning a small area to benefit a single property owner
C. Zoning that changes frequently
D. Zoning based on environmental impact

Answer: B

Spot zoning is the application of zoning to a specific parcel or parcels of land within a larger zoned area when the rezoning is usually at odds with a city's master plan.

➡ **25. What is "air rights"?**

   A. The right to unlimited height in construction

   B. The right to the space above a property

   C. The right to pollute the air

   D. The right to air grievances in a public forum

Answer: B

Air rights refer to the empty space above a property; owning the air rights means you control the use of this space.

➡ **26. What is the primary purpose of a "variance" in zoning?**

   A. To change the zoning code

   B. To allow a specific exception to the zoning rules

   C. To increase property taxes

   D. To decrease property taxes

Answer: B

A variance is a request to deviate from current zoning requirements, usually because the zoning ordinance would bring unnecessary hardship to a specific property.

➡ **27. What does "eminent domain" refer to?**

   A. The right of the government to tax property

   B. The right of the government to seize private property for public use

   C. The right of the property owner to change zoning laws

   D. The right of the property owner to refuse sale to the government

Answer: B

Eminent domain is the right of a government to take private property for public use, usually with compensation to the owner.

→28. What is the primary purpose of a "buffer zone" in land use planning?

A. To separate residential and commercial areas
B. To provide space for public parks
C. To reduce noise pollution
D. To increase property values

Answer: A

A buffer zone is often used to separate different types of land uses, such as residential and commercial areas, to minimize conflicts and improve the quality of life for residents.

→29. What is the "highest and best use" principle?

A. The most profitable use of a property
B. The use that generates the most tax revenue
C. The use that is most suitable and likely to be supported by the community
D. The use that is most environmentally sustainable

Answer: A

The "highest and best use" is the most profitable, legally permitted, feasible, and physically possible use of a property.

→30. What is "buffer zoning"?

A. Zoning that allows for any type of use
B. Zoning that separates residential areas from commercial areas
C. Zoning that protects natural resources
D. Zoning that allows for mixed-use development

Answer: B

Buffer zoning is used to transition between residential and more intense uses like commercial or industrial zones, often using green spaces, fences, or other buffers.

➡ 31. What is "bulk zoning"?

    A. Zoning based on building size

    B. Zoning based on land area

    C. Zoning that allows for any type of use

    D. Zoning that restricts the height of buildings

Answer: A

Bulk zoning regulates the height, mass, and size of buildings.

➡ 32. What is "floor area ratio (FAR)"?

    A. The ratio of a building's total floor area to the size of the piece of land upon which it is built

    B. The ratio of the building's height to its width

    C. The ratio of commercial to residential area in a building

    D. The ratio of the building's footprint to its total floor area

Answer: A

The floor area ratio (FAR) is the ratio of a building's total floor area to the size of the land upon which it is built.

➡ 33. What is "contract zoning"?

    A. Zoning based on a legal agreement between the property owner and the municipality

    B. Zoning that changes frequently

    C. Zoning that is determined by a vote

    D. Zoning that is the same for an entire city

Answer: A

Contract zoning is a legal agreement between a property owner and a municipality regarding the use of the property.

➡ **34. What is "form-based zoning"?**

    A. Zoning based on building function

    B. Zoning based on building form

    C. Zoning based on land use

    D. Zoning based on environmental impact

Answer: B

Form-based zoning regulates the form, scale, and appearance of development, rather than only the use.

➡ **35. What is "conditional use permit"?**

    A. A permit that allows for a change in zoning

    B. A permit that allows a use not normally permitted in a zone

    C. A permit that allows for temporary use of a property

    D. A permit that allows for the subdivision of land

Answer: B

A conditional use permit allows a use that is not normally permitted in a zone but is allowed under certain conditions.

➡ **36. What is the primary function of a "master plan" in city planning?**

    A. To outline future development and land use

    B. To set tax rates for different zones

    C. To allocate funds for public services

    D. To regulate current land use only

Answer: A

A master plan is designed to guide the future development and land use of a city or area, including the placement of various types of buildings, transportation systems, and public spaces.

➡37. What does the term "infill development" refer to?

    A. Developing open spaces in urban areas

    B. Developing land in rural areas

    C. Developing land in suburban areas

    D. Developing land in protected areas

Answer: A

Infill development refers to the development of vacant or underused parcels within existing urban areas that are already largely developed.

➡38. What does "downzoning" typically result in?

    A. Higher density development

    B. Lower density development

    C. No change in density

    D. Increased commercial development

Answer: B

Downzoning typically results in lower density development, often changing zones from commercial or high-density residential to lower-density residential.

➡39. What is the main purpose of a "variance" in zoning?

    A. To change the zoning laws

    B. To allow a specific exception to zoning laws

    C. To increase property taxes

D. To decrease property taxes

A variance is a request to deviate from current zoning requirements. If granted, it allows the property to be used in a way that is normally not permitted by the zoning ordinance.

➡️**40. What does "by-right development" mean?**

    A. Development that is automatically approved

    B. Development that requires special permission

    C. Development that is prohibited

    D. Development that requires a public vote

Answer: A

By-right development refers to development activities that are allowed under the current zoning and land use regulations and therefore do not require special approval.

➡️**41. What is "mixed-use development"?**

    A. Development for industrial use only

    B. Development for residential use only

    C. Development that includes various types of uses

    D. Development for commercial use only

Answer: C

Mixed-use development includes a mixture of land uses within a single development, community, or area.

➡️**42. What is "upzoning"?**

    A. Changing a zone to allow for more dense development

    B. Changing a zone to allow for less dense development

C. Changing a zone to commercial use

D. Changing a zone to residential use

Answer: A

Upzoning is the practice of changing the zoning on a piece of land to allow for more dense development.

➡️43. What does "exclusionary zoning" primarily aim to do?

A. Include multiple types of land uses

B. Exclude certain types of land uses

C. Promote industrial development

D. Promote residential development

Answer: B

Exclusionary zoning is the economic segregation that is the result of zoning ordinances that prevent certain types of land uses in a given community.

➡️44. What does "floor area ratio (FAR)" measure?

A. The ratio of a building's total floor area to the size of the piece of land upon which it is built

B. The ratio of commercial to residential space in a building

C. The ratio of a building's height to its width

D. The ratio of green space to built space in a development

Answer: A

Floor Area Ratio (FAR) is the ratio of a building's total floor area to the size of the piece of land upon which it is built. It is often used in zoning codes to control density.

➡️45. What is "greenfield development"?

A. Development on previously undeveloped land

B. Development focused on environmental sustainability

C. Development in urban areas

D. Development in industrial zones

Answer: A

Greenfield development refers to construction on land that has never been used, where there is no need to remodel or demolish an existing structure.

➡46. What is "brownfield development"?

A. Development on agricultural land

B. Development on previously developed land that may be contaminated

C. Development in forested areas

D. Development in commercial zones

Answer: B

Brownfield development refers to the development or redevelopment of land which has been previously used and may be contaminated with hazardous waste or pollution.

➡47. What does "transit-oriented development" aim to achieve?

A. Reduce reliance on public transport

B. Increase reliance on cars

C. Increase the use of public transport

D. Promote rural development

Answer: C

Transit-oriented development aims to maximize the amount of residential, business, and leisure space within walking distance of public transport to reduce the need for cars.

➡48. What is "eminent domain"?

A. The right of a government to take private property for public use

B. The right of a property owner to develop land as they see fit

C. The right of a tenant to purchase rented property

D. The right of a government to tax property

Answer: A

Eminent domain is the right of a government or its agent to expropriate private property for public use, with payment of compensation.

➡**49. What is "restrictive covenant"?**

A. A legal obligation imposed in a lease

B. A restriction on the use of land so that the value and enjoyment of adjoining land are preserved

C. A restriction on the height of buildings

D. A restriction on the types of businesses that can operate in a certain area

Answer: B

A restrictive covenant is a clause in a deed or lease that limits what the owner of the land or lease can do with the property.

➡**50. What is "land banking"?**

A. The process of buying land as an investment

B. The process of rezoning land

C. The process of converting agricultural land for urban use

D. The process of land conservation

Answer: A

Land banking is the practice of aggregating parcels of land for future sale or development.

Laws of Agency and Fiduciary Duties

The concept of agency is the bedrock upon which all real estate transactions in Texas are built. It's not just about buying and selling; it's about trust, responsibility, and legal obligations. This chapter aims to offer an exhaustive look into the laws of agency and fiduciary duties, which are the cornerstones of ethical and legal real estate practice in Texas.

What is Agency?

Agency is a legal construct that allows one individual to act on behalf of another. In the realm of real estate, this often means a broker or salesperson acting on behalf of a client, who could be a buyer, seller, landlord, or tenant.

Types of Agency Relationships

Seller's Agent: Solely represents the seller and owes fiduciary duties to the seller alone.

Buyer's Agent: Exclusively represents the buyer's interests.

Dual Agent: Represents both parties, requiring explicit consent from both the buyer and the seller.

Subagent: An agent of an agent, often a situation found in larger brokerages.

Transaction Broker: A neutral party facilitating the transaction without representing either side.

The Complexity of Dual Agency

Dual agency is a complex arrangement that can lead to ethical dilemmas. The agent must balance the interests of both parties, which can be particularly challenging when it comes to negotiations over price and terms.

Fiduciary Duties

Fiduciary duties are the set of responsibilities that an agent owes to their principal. These duties are not merely guidelines but are legally enforceable obligations.

The Six Core Fiduciary Duties

Loyalty: Unwavering allegiance to the principal's interests.

Obedience: Following all lawful instructions.

Disclosure: Revealing all material facts.

Confidentiality: Protecting the principal's private information.

Accounting: Keeping accurate records of all transactions.

Reasonable Care: Exercising competence and diligence.

The Nuances of Disclosure

Disclosure isn't just about revealing defects in a property; it's also about disclosing any personal relationships or benefits that could influence the agent's recommendations. For instance, if the agent stands to gain a bonus or gift for selling a particular property, this must be disclosed to the principal.

Legal Framework

The Texas Real Estate License Act (TRELA) and the Texas Real Estate Commission (TREC) provide the legal framework for agency relationships. These laws are not static; they evolve to reflect changes in the industry and society at large.

Importance of Written Agreements

In Texas, oral agreements are not sufficient to establish an agency relationship in real estate transactions. Written agreements protect both the agent and the principal by clearly outlining roles, responsibilities, and compensation.

Risks and Liabilities

Non-compliance with fiduciary duties can result in severe repercussions, including legal action, fines, and even revocation of the agent's license.

Real-world Case Studies

Breach of Confidentiality: An agent in Texas was sued for revealing a client's divorce status, which led to a lower offer on a property.

Failure to Disclose: An agent failed to disclose that a property was in a flood zone, resulting in a lawsuit when the property flooded.

Conclusion

The laws of agency and fiduciary duties are not just rules to follow; they are the ethical backbone of the real estate profession in Texas. Understanding and adhering to these laws is not only crucial for passing the Texas Real Estate License Exam but also for building a successful, reputable career in real estate.

Mock Exam Laws of Agency and Fiduciary Duties

➡1. What is the primary legal document that establishes an agency relationship in Texas real estate transactions?

    A. Listing Agreement

    B. Buyer Representation Agreement

    C. Both A and B

    D. None of the above

Answer: C

Both the Listing Agreement and Buyer Representation Agreement are primary legal documents that establish an agency relationship in Texas.

➡2. Which of the following is NOT a core fiduciary duty?

    A. Loyalty

    B. Disclosure

    C. Commission

    D. Confidentiality

Answer: C

Commission is not a fiduciary duty; it is a form of compensation for the agent.

➡3. What is dual agency?

    A. Representing only the buyer

    B. Representing only the seller

    C. Representing both the buyer and the seller

    D. Representing neither the buyer nor the seller

Answer: C

Dual agency refers to an agent representing both the buyer and the seller in a real estate transaction.

➡4. What organization provides the legal framework for agency relationships in Texas?

    A. NAR

    B. TRELA

    C. TREC

    D. MLS

Answer: B

The Texas Real Estate License Act (TRELA) provides the legal framework for agency relationships in Texas.

➡5. What is the penalty for breaching fiduciary duties?

    A. A warning

    B. Legal action and fines

    C. Revocation of license

    D. Both B and C

Answer: D

Breaching fiduciary duties can result in legal action, fines, and even revocation of the agent's license.

➡6. Which of the following is **NOT** a type of agency relationship?

    A. Seller's Agent

    B. Buyer's Agent

C. Transaction Broker

D. Mortgage Broker

Answer: D

A Mortgage Broker is not a type of agency relationship in real estate; they deal with loan origination.

➡7. What is the fiduciary duty of obedience?

    A. Following all lawful instructions

    B. Revealing all material facts

    C. Protecting the principal's private information

    D. Keeping accurate records of all transactions

Answer: A

The fiduciary duty of obedience involves following all lawful instructions from the principal.

➡8. What must be disclosed according to the fiduciary duty of disclosure?

    A. Only property defects

    B. All material facts

    C. Only personal relationships

    D. Only financial benefits

Answer: B

The fiduciary duty of disclosure requires revealing all material facts, not just property defects.

➡9. What type of agency relationship requires explicit consent from both parties?

    A. Seller's Agent

    B. Buyer's Agent

C. Dual Agent

D. Subagent

Answer: C

Dual agency requires explicit consent from both the buyer and the seller.

➠10. **What is the role of a subagent?**

  A. To represent the buyer

  B. To represent the seller

  C. To facilitate the transaction

  D. To act as an agent of the agent

Answer: D

A subagent acts as an agent of the agent, often found in larger brokerages.

➠11. **What is the primary purpose of a fiduciary duty?**

  A. To protect the agent

  B. To protect the principal

  C. To protect the broker

  D. To protect the transaction

Answer: B

The primary purpose of a fiduciary duty is to protect the interests of the principal in the agency relationship.

➠12. **What is the difference between a general agent and a special agent?**

  A. Scope of authority

  B. Duration of relationship

  C. Type of property

D. Commission rate

Answer: A

A general agent has broader authority and responsibilities, while a special agent has limited, specific tasks.

➡️**13. What is the fiduciary duty of accounting?**

A. Keeping accurate financial records

B. Disclosing all material facts

C. Following lawful instructions

D. Maintaining confidentiality

Answer: A

The fiduciary duty of accounting involves keeping accurate financial records related to the transaction.

➡️**14. What is the legal consequence of undisclosed dual agency?**

A. A fine

B. Revocation of license

C. Legal action

D. All of the above

Answer: D

Undisclosed dual agency can result in a fine, legal action, and even revocation of the agent's license.

➡️**15. What is the fiduciary duty of care?**

A. To act with competence

B. To disclose all material facts

C. To follow lawful instructions

D. To protect the principal's interests

Answer: A

The fiduciary duty of care involves acting with competence and skill in representing the principal.

➡16. What does the term "imputed knowledge" refer to in an agency relationship?

    A. Knowledge shared between agents

    B. Knowledge assumed by the principal

    C. Knowledge that the agent should have

    D. Knowledge that is confidential

Answer: A

Imputed knowledge refers to the sharing of information between agents in the same brokerage.

➡17. What is the primary role of the Texas Real Estate Commission (TREC)?

    A. To enforce real estate laws

    B. To provide educational resources

    C. To issue licenses

    D. All of the above

Answer: D

TREC is responsible for enforcing real estate laws, providing educational resources, and issuing licenses.

➡18. What is the fiduciary duty of loyalty?

    A. To act in the best interest of the principal

B. To disclose all material facts

C. To follow lawful instructions

D. To keep accurate financial records

Answer: A

The fiduciary duty of loyalty involves acting in the best interest of the principal.

➡19. What is the primary purpose of the Information About Brokerage Services form?

A. To disclose agency relationships

B. To outline commission rates

C. To provide contact information

D. To list available properties

Answer: A

The form is primarily used to disclose agency relationships to the parties involved.

➡20. What is the fiduciary duty of confidentiality?

A. To protect the principal's private information

B. To disclose all material facts

C. To follow lawful instructions

D. To keep accurate financial records

Answer: A

The fiduciary duty of confidentiality involves protecting the principal's private information.

➡21. What is the primary duty of a fiduciary agent to their client?

A. To maximize profit for themselves

B. To disclose all known facts about a property

C. To act in the best interest of the client

D. To find the client the cheapest property available

Answer: C

The primary duty of a fiduciary agent is to act in the best interest of their client, putting the client's needs above their own.

➡️**22. What is the fiduciary duty of disclosure?**

A. To protect the principal's private information

B. To disclose all material facts

C. To follow lawful instructions

D. To keep accurate financial records

Answer: B

The fiduciary duty of disclosure requires the agent to disclose all material facts that could affect the transaction.

➡️**23. What is the role of a sub-agent?**

A. To represent the buyer

B. To represent the seller

C. To represent the broker

D. To represent the principal

Answer: D

A sub-agent is an agent of the original agent and, therefore, also represents the principal.

➡️**24. What is the difference between express and implied agency?**

A. Written vs. Verbal

B. Formal vs. Informal

C. Explicit vs. Assumed

D. Short-term vs. Long-term

Answer: C

Express agency is explicitly agreed upon, while implied agency is assumed based on the behavior of the parties.

➡**25. What is the primary purpose of the Consumer Protection Notice?**

A. To disclose agency relationships

B. To outline commission rates

C. To provide contact information

D. To inform consumers of their rights and obligations

Answer: D

The Consumer Protection Notice is designed to inform consumers of their rights and obligations under Texas real estate law.

➡**26. What is the fiduciary duty of reasonable care?**

A. To act with competence

B. To disclose all material facts

C. To follow lawful instructions

D. To protect the principal's interests

Answer: A

The fiduciary duty of reasonable care involves acting with competence and skill in representing the principal.

➡**27. What is the role of a transaction broker?**

A. To represent the buyer

B. To represent the seller

C. To facilitate the transaction

D. To represent the principal

Answer: C

A transaction broker's role is to facilitate the transaction without representing either party.

➡ **28. What is the fiduciary duty of indemnification?**

A. To protect the principal from financial loss

B. To disclose all material facts

C. To follow lawful instructions

D. To keep accurate financial records

Answer: A

The fiduciary duty of indemnification involves protecting the principal from financial loss related to the agent's actions.

➡ **29. What is the primary role of the Texas Real Estate Commission's Recovery Trust Account?**

A. To provide educational resources

B. To compensate aggrieved parties

C. To enforce real estate laws

D. To issue licenses

Answer: B

The Recovery Trust Account is primarily used to compensate aggrieved parties who suffer financial loss due to a licensee's actions.

➡ **30. What is the fiduciary duty of honesty?**

A. To act truthfully

B. To disclose all material facts

C. To follow lawful instructions

D. To protect the principal's interests

Answer: A

The fiduciary duty of honesty requires the agent to act truthfully in all dealings with the principal.

➡**31. What is the term for when an agent represents both the buyer and the seller in a single transaction?**

A. Dual Agency

B. Single Agency

C. Subagency

D. Designated Agency

Answer: A

Dual Agency refers to the practice where the same agent represents both the buyer and the seller in a single transaction.

➡**32. What is the primary purpose of a buyer's agent?**

A. To list properties

B. To represent the seller

C. To represent the buyer

D. To act as a neutral party

Answer: C

The primary purpose of a buyer's agent is to represent the interests of the buyer in a real estate transaction.

➡33. What is the term for the legal relationship between a principal and an agent?

    A. Contract

    B. Fiduciary

    C. Partnership

    D. Employment

Answer: B

The term for the legal relationship between a principal and an agent is a fiduciary relationship.

➡34. What must an agent do if they receive multiple offers on a property?

    A. Accept the highest offer immediately

    B. Present all offers to the seller

    C. Choose the offer that benefits them most

    D. Discard lower offers

Answer: B

An agent is obligated to present all offers to the seller for consideration.

➡35. What is the term for an agent who is working for a broker?

    A. Subagent

    B. Associate broker

    C. Salesperson

    D. Dual agent

Answer: C

An agent working for a broker is commonly referred to as a salesperson.

➡36. What is the primary role of a listing agent?

    A. To find properties for buyers

    B. To represent the seller

    C. To represent the buyer

    D. To act as a neutral party

Answer: B

The primary role of a listing agent is to represent the seller in a real estate transaction.

➡37. What is required for an agency relationship to be terminated?

    A. Mutual agreement

    B. Written notice

    C. Completion of the transaction

    D. All of the above

Answer: D

An agency relationship can be terminated through mutual agreement, written notice, or the completion of the transaction for which the agency was formed.

➡38. What is the term for an agent who represents the buyer but is paid by the seller?

    A. Dual agent

    B. Subagent

    C. Buyer's agent

    D. Transaction broker

Answer: B

A subagent is an agent who represents the buyer but is paid by the seller.

39. What is the term for a broker who represents neither the buyer nor the seller but facilitates the transaction?

  A. Transaction broker

  B. Dual agent

  C. Subagent

  D. Listing agent

Answer: A

A transaction broker facilitates the transaction without representing either party.

40. What is the term for a written agreement between a seller and an agent?

  A. Purchase agreement

  B. Listing agreement

  C. Buyer's agreement

  D. Lease agreement

Answer: B

A listing agreement is a written contract between a seller and an agent outlining the terms under which the agent will work to sell the property.

41. What is the term for a broker who is working under another broker?

  A. Subagent

  B. Associate broker

  C. Salesperson

  D. Dual agent

Answer: B

An associate broker is a licensed broker who chooses to work under the management of another broker.

→42. What is the primary duty of a fiduciary?

   A. To make a profit
   B. To act in the best interest of the principal
   C. To find buyers
   D. To list properties

Answer: B

The primary duty of a fiduciary is to act in the best interest of the principal.

→43. What is a "pocket listing"?

   A. A listing that is not yet on the MLS
   B. A listing that is only available to certain agents
   C. A listing that has been sold
   D. A listing that is under contract

Answer: A

A "pocket listing" is a listing that is not yet publicly advertised on the MLS.

→44. What is the term for a situation where an agent puts their interests above those of the principal?

   A. Breach of duty
   B. Dual agency
   C. Subagency
   D. Negligence

Answer: A

Putting one's interests above those of the principal is considered a breach of fiduciary duty.

→45. What is the term for the document that outlines the specific tasks an agent will perform for a buyer?

    A. Buyer's agreement

    B. Listing agreement

    C. Contract of sale

    D. Lease agreement

Answer: A

A Buyer's Agreement outlines the specific tasks an agent will perform for a buyer.

→46. What is the term for a broker who represents only the buyer or only the seller but not both?

    A. Single agency

    B. Dual agency

    C. Subagency

    D. Transaction broker

Answer: A

Single agency is when a broker represents only one party in a transaction, either the buyer or the seller.

→47. What is the term for an agent who is authorized to perform a single act for a principal?

    A. Special agent

    B. General agent

    C. Universal agent

D. Dual agent

Answer: A

A Special Agent is authorized to perform a single act for a principal.

➡**48. What is the term for an agent who is authorized to represent a principal in all matters?**

    A. Special agent
    B. General agent
    C. Universal agent
    D. Dual agent

Answer: C

A Universal Agent is authorized to represent a principal in all matters.

➡**49. What is the term for an agent who is authorized to represent a principal in a range of matters related to a specific business?**

    A. Special agent
    B. General agent
    C. Universal agent
    D. Dual agent

Answer: B

A General Agent is authorized to represent a principal in a range of matters related to a specific business.

➡**50. What is the term for a situation where an agent represents a buyer but is subordinated to the seller's agent?**

A. Single agency

B. Dual agency

C. Subagency

D. Transaction broker

Answer: C

Subagency is when an agent represents a buyer but is subordinated to the seller's agent.

Property Valuation and Financial Analysis

The real estate market is a complex ecosystem where property valuation and financial analysis play pivotal roles. Whether you're an investor, a real estate agent, or a prospective homeowner, understanding the intricacies of these concepts is crucial for making informed decisions. This chapter aims to provide an in-depth understanding of the various methods and financial metrics used in property valuation.

Types of Valuation Methods

Comparative Market Analysis (CMA)

CMA is the cornerstone of residential property valuation. It involves a detailed comparison of the property in question with similar properties that have recently sold, are currently on the market, or were listed but did not sell. Factors such as location, size, condition, and unique features are considered. The CMA process often involves adjustments for differences between the subject property and comparables, providing a more accurate valuation.

Importance of CMA
CMA is particularly useful for sellers to set a realistic selling price and for buyers to ensure they are not overpaying for a property. Real estate agents often provide a CMA as part of their service to clients.

- Cost Approach

The cost approach is often used for new or unique properties where comparable sales data may not be available. This method calculates the cost to replace the property, considering the current price of land and the cost of construction, less any depreciation.

Factors in Cost Approach
- *Land Cost:* The current market value of the land.

- *Construction Cost:* Includes labor and material costs.
- *Depreciation:* Physical, functional, and economic depreciation are considered.

- Income Capitalization Approach

This method is commonly used for commercial and investment properties. It involves calculating the Net Operating Income (NOI) the property is expected to generate and then using a capitalization rate to find the property's value.

Steps in Income Capitalization

1. Estimate potential gross income.

2. Deduct operating expenses.

3. Apply the capitalization rate.

- Discounted Cash Flow (DCF)

For properties expected to generate future income, the DCF method is often used. It involves estimating the future cash flows and discounting them back to their present value using a discount rate, often the investor's required rate of return.

DCF Variables

- *Cash inflows and outflows*
- *Discount rate*
- *Holding period*

Key Financial Metrics

Return on Investment (ROI)

ROI is a universal metric that measures the profitability of an investment. It is calculated by dividing the net profit by the initial investment cost. ROI is expressed as a percentage and is useful for comparing the profitability of different investment opportunities.

Capitalization Rate (Cap Rate)

Cap rate is a key metric used to evaluate the potential return on an investment property. It is calculated by dividing the NOI by the current market value of the property. A higher cap rate usually indicates a higher potential return but also comes with higher risk.

Cash on Cash Return

This metric is particularly useful for properties that require a down payment and a mortgage. It calculates the cash income earned on the cash invested in a property, providing a more accurate picture of an investment's performance.

Debt Service Coverage Ratio (DSCR)

DSCR is a critical metric for lenders. It measures the property's ability to cover its debt obligations. A DSCR of less than 1 indicates that the property is not generating enough income to cover its debts, making it a risky investment.

Net Present Value (NPV) and Internal Rate of Return (IRR)

NPV and IRR are advanced metrics used in DCF analysis. While NPV provides a dollar value that represents the profitability of an investment, IRR provides the annualized rate of return. Both are critical for investment analysis and are often used in tandem.

Conclusion

Property valuation and financial analysis are not just theoretical concepts but practical tools that every real estate professional should master. This chapter has aimed to provide a comprehensive, in-depth understanding of these critical aspects of real estate. Whether you're an investor looking for a profitable opportunity, a real estate agent aiming to provide the best service to your clients, or a buyer looking to make the most significant investment of your life, understanding these concepts is not just beneficial—it's essential.

Mock Exam Property Valuation and Financial Analysis

➡ **1. What is the primary purpose of Comparative Market Analysis (CMA)?**

   A. To estimate construction costs

   B. To calculate Net Operating Income

   C. To set a realistic selling price

   D. To calculate the capitalization rate

Answer: C

The primary purpose of CMA is to set a realistic selling price for a property by comparing it with similar properties that have recently sold, are currently on the market, or were listed but did not sell.

➡ **2. Which of the following is NOT a type of depreciation considered in the Cost Approach?**

   A. Physical

   B. Functional

   C. Emotional

   D. Economic

Answer: C

Emotional depreciation is not a recognized form of depreciation in the Cost Approach. The types considered are Physical, Functional, and Economic.

➡ **3. What does ROI stand for?**

   A. Rate of Investment

   B. Return on Investment

   C. Realistic Operating Income

D. Rate of Inflation

Answer: B

ROI stands for Return on Investment. It measures the profitability of an investment.

➡️**4. What is the formula for calculating the Capitalization Rate (Cap Rate)?**

A. NOI / Current Market Value

B. Current Market Value / NOI

C. NOI * Current Market Value

D. Current Market Value - NOI

Answer: A

The formula for calculating the Capitalization Rate is NOI divided by the current market value of the property.

➡️**5. Which valuation method is commonly used for commercial and investment properties?**

A. Comparative Market Analysis

B. Cost Approach

C. Income Capitalization Approach

D. Discounted Cash Flow

Answer: C

The Income Capitalization Approach is commonly used for commercial and investment properties to calculate their value based on the Net Operating Income they are expected to generate.

➡️**6. What does DSCR stand for?**

A. Debt Service Capital Ratio

B. Debt Service Coverage Ratio

C. Debt Security Coverage Rate

D. Debt Service Capital Rate

Answer: B

DSCR stands for Debt Service Coverage Ratio. It measures the property's ability to cover its debt obligations.

➡ **7. What is the primary variable in the Discounted Cash Flow (DCF) method?**

A. Cash inflows and outflows

B. Capitalization Rate

C. Comparative Market Analysis

D. Construction Costs

Answer: A

The primary variable in the DCF method is the estimation of future cash inflows and outflows from the property.

➡ **8. What is the formula for calculating ROI?**

A. (Net Profit / Initial Investment Cost) * 100

B. (Initial Investment Cost / Net Profit) * 100

C. Net Profit - Initial Investment Cost

D. Initial Investment Cost - Net Profit

Answer: A

The formula for calculating ROI is (Net Profit divided by Initial Investment Cost) multiplied by 100.

➡ **9. Which of the following is NOT a step in the Income Capitalization Approach?**

A. Estimate potential gross income

B. Deduct operating expenses

C. Calculate the discount rate

D. Apply the capitalization rate

Answer: C

Calculating the discount rate is not a step in the Income Capitalization Approach. The steps include estimating potential gross income, deducting operating expenses, and applying the capitalization rate.

➡10. What does NPV stand for?

A. Net Present Value

B. Net Profit Value

C. New Property Value

D. Net Price Valuation

Answer: A

NPV stands for Net Present Value. It provides a dollar value that represents the profitability of an investment.

➡11. What is the primary purpose of a Gross Rent Multiplier (GRM)?

A. To estimate property taxes

B. To evaluate the profitability of a rental property

C. To calculate the capitalization rate

D. To assess the market value of a property

Answer: B

The primary purpose of a Gross Rent Multiplier is to evaluate the profitability of a rental property by comparing the property's price to its gross rental income.

➡12. What does LTV stand for?

A. Loan To Value

B. Long-Term Valuation

C. Loan To Vendor

D. Lease To Value

Answer: A

LTV stands for Loan To Value. It is a ratio that compares the amount of a loan to the value of the property being purchased.

➡️**13. What is the formula for calculating Net Operating Income (NOI)?**

A. Gross Income - Operating Expenses

B. Gross Income + Operating Expenses

C. Operating Expenses - Gross Income

D. Operating Expenses / Gross Income

Answer: A

The formula for calculating Net Operating Income is Gross Income minus Operating Expenses.

➡️**14. Which of the following is NOT a factor in the Sales Comparison Approach?**

A. Location

B. Size

C. Color

D. Age

Answer: C

Color is not a factor considered in the Sales Comparison Approach. Factors like location, size, and age are considered.

➡️**15. What is the purpose of a cap rate?**

A. To set rent prices

B. To evaluate the risk and potential return of an investment property

C. To calculate property taxes

D. To determine the interest rate of a mortgage

Answer: B

The purpose of a cap rate is to evaluate the risk and potential return of an investment property.

➡16. **What does the term "amortization" refer to?**

A. The process of increasing property value

B. The process of paying off a loan over time

C. The process of calculating property taxes

D. The process of estimating repair costs

Answer: B

Amortization refers to the process of paying off a loan over time through regular payments.

➡17. **What is the formula for calculating Gross Rent Multiplier (GRM)?**

A. Property Price / Monthly Rent

B. Monthly Rent / Property Price

C. Property Price * Monthly Rent

D. Monthly Rent - Property Price

Answer: A

The formula for calculating Gross Rent Multiplier is Property Price divided by Monthly Rent.

➡18. **What is the primary purpose of a feasibility study in real estate?**

A. To evaluate the potential success of a real estate project

B. To calculate the capitalization rate

C. To set a realistic selling price

D. To estimate construction costs

Answer: A

The primary purpose of a feasibility study is to evaluate the potential success of a real estate project.

➡ **19. What does the term "liquidity" refer to in real estate investment?**

A. The ease with which an asset can be converted into cash

B. The profitability of an investment

C. The risk associated with an investment

D. The long-term value of an asset

Answer: A

In real estate investment, liquidity refers to the ease with which an asset can be converted into cash.

➡ **20. What is the formula for calculating Loan-to-Value (LTV) ratio?**

A. (Loan Amount / Property Value) * 100

B. (Property Value / Loan Amount) * 100

C. Loan Amount - Property Value

D. Property Value - Loan Amount

Answer: A

The formula for calculating Loan-to-Value ratio is (Loan Amount divided by Property Value) multiplied by 100.

21. What is the Debt Service Coverage Ratio (DSCR) primarily used for?

    A. To evaluate the liquidity of an investment

    B. To assess a borrower's ability to cover loan payments

    C. To calculate property taxes

    D. To determine the market value of a property

Answer: B

The Debt Service Coverage Ratio (DSCR) is primarily used to assess a borrower's ability to cover loan payments from the property's net operating income.

22. What does the term "equity" refer to in real estate?

    A. The difference between the property's market value and the outstanding loan balance

    B. The total value of the property

    C. The initial down payment

    D. The annual rent income

Answer: A

Equity refers to the difference between the property's market value and the outstanding loan balance.

23. What is a "balloon payment"?

    A. A small, initial down payment

    B. A large, final payment at the end of a loan term

    C. A monthly mortgage payment

    D. An annual property tax payment

Answer: B

A balloon payment is a large, final payment that comes due at the end of a loan term.

➥24. What is the primary purpose of a pro forma statement in real estate?

   A. To provide a historical record of a property's income and expenses

   B. To provide a future projection of a property's income and expenses

   C. To calculate the property's current market value

   D. To assess the risk associated with an investment

Answer: B

The primary purpose of a pro forma statement is to provide a future projection of a property's income and expenses.

➥25. What does the term "underwriting" refer to in real estate financing?

   A. The process of evaluating the risk of insuring a home

   B. The process of evaluating a borrower's creditworthiness

   C. The process of setting rent prices

   D. The process of calculating property taxes

Answer: B

Underwriting refers to the process of evaluating a borrower's creditworthiness for a mortgage loan.

➥26. What is the formula for calculating Capitalization Rate (Cap Rate)?

   A. Net Operating Income / Property Value

   B. Property Value / Net Operating Income

   C. Net Operating Income * Property Value

   D. Property Value - Net Operating Income

Answer: A

The formula for calculating Capitalization Rate is Net Operating Income divided by Property Value.

➡ 27. What is the primary purpose of a Comparative Market Analysis (CMA)?

    A. To set rent prices

    B. To evaluate the risk and potential return of an investment property

    C. To estimate the market value of a property

    D. To calculate property taxes

Answer: C

The primary purpose of a Comparative Market Analysis is to estimate the market value of a property.

➡ 28. What is the "time value of money" concept?

    A. Money available today is worth more than the same amount in the future

    B. Money loses value over time due to inflation

    C. Money gains value over time due to interest

    D. Money's value remains constant over time

Answer: A

The "time value of money" concept states that money available today is worth more than the same amount in the future.

➡ 29. What does the term "due diligence" refer to in real estate?

    A. The process of evaluating a property before purchase

    B. The process of setting rent prices

    C. The process of calculating property taxes

    D. The process of applying for a mortgage

Answer: A

Due diligence refers to the process of thoroughly evaluating a property before making a purchase.

➠30. What is a "contingency" in a real estate contract?

   A. A penalty for late payment

   B. A condition that must be met for the contract to proceed

   C. A fixed interest rate

   D. A non-refundable deposit

Answer: B

A contingency is a condition that must be met for the real estate contract to proceed.

➠31. What is the Gross Rent Multiplier (GRM)?

   A. Property Value / Monthly Rent

   B. Monthly Rent / Property Value

   C. Annual Rent / Property Value

   D. Property Value / Annual Rent

Answer: A

The Gross Rent Multiplier (GRM) is calculated by dividing the property value by the monthly rent. It's used to evaluate the value of an income-producing property.

➠32. What does Loan-to-Value (LTV) ratio represent?

   A. The ratio of the loan amount to the borrower's income

   B. The ratio of the loan amount to the property's appraised value

   C. The ratio of the property's appraised value to the loan amount

   D. The ratio of the borrower's income to the loan amount

Answer: B

The Loan-to-Value (LTV) ratio represents the ratio of the loan amount to the property's appraised value.

➡33. What is the purpose of a "good faith estimate"?

    A. To provide an estimate of closing costs

    B. To estimate the property's market value

    C. To provide an estimate of monthly mortgage payments

    D. To estimate annual property taxes

Answer: A

The purpose of a "good faith estimate" is to provide an estimate of the closing costs associated with a mortgage loan.

➡34. What does "amortization" mean in the context of a mortgage?

    A. The process of increasing the loan amount

    B. The process of paying off the loan over time through regular payments

    C. The process of adjusting the interest rate

    D. The process of refinancing the loan

Answer: B

Amortization refers to the process of paying off a loan over time through regular payments that cover both principal and interest.

➡35. What is a "cash-on-cash return"?

    A. The ratio of annual net income to total investment

    B. The ratio of annual net income to property value

    C. The ratio of monthly rent to property value

    D. The ratio of property value to annual net income

Answer: A

Cash-on-cash return is the ratio of annual net income to the total investment made in the property.

⇒36. What is "negative gearing"?

    A. When rental income exceeds property expenses

    B. When property expenses exceed rental income

    C. When the property value increases

    D. When the property value decreases

Answer: B

Negative gearing occurs when the property expenses exceed the rental income, resulting in a loss that can often be offset against other income for tax purposes.

⇒37. What is an "escrow account" commonly used for?

    A. To hold the security deposit

    B. To hold funds for property taxes and insurance

    C. To hold the down payment

    D. To hold funds for property repairs

Answer: B

An escrow account is commonly used to hold funds that will be used to pay property taxes and insurance.

⇒38. What does "yield" refer to in real estate investment?

    A. The annual rent as a percentage of property value

    B. The property value as a percentage of annual rent

    C. The monthly mortgage payment as a percentage of property value

    D. The property value as a percentage of the loan amount

Answer: A

Yield refers to the annual rent as a percentage of the property value, and it's used to evaluate the return on investment.

39. What is a "jumbo loan"?

A. A loan that is smaller than the conforming loan limits

B. A loan that exceeds conforming loan limits

C. A loan with a very low interest rate

D. A loan with a very high interest rate

Answer: B

A jumbo loan is a type of mortgage that exceeds the conforming loan limits set by government-sponsored agencies.

40. What is "leverage" in real estate investment?

A. The use of borrowed funds to increase potential return

B. The ratio of debt to equity

C. The ratio of property value to loan amount

D. The use of personal funds to avoid taking a loan

Answer: A

Leverage in real estate investment refers to the use of borrowed funds to increase the potential return on an investment.

41. What is the primary purpose of a "cap rate"?

A. To determine the property's appreciation rate

B. To evaluate the profitability of an investment property

C. To calculate the monthly mortgage payment

D. To assess the risk of loan default

Answer: B

The capitalization rate, or cap rate, is used to evaluate the profitability of an investment property. It is calculated by dividing the property's net operating income by its current market value.

➧42. What does "equity" mean in the context of real estate?

A. The value of the property minus the outstanding mortgage

B. The outstanding mortgage minus the value of the property

C. The annual rent income

D. The total amount of mortgage payments made

Answer: A

Equity refers to the value of the property minus the outstanding mortgage. It represents the homeowner's ownership stake in the property.

➧43. What does "amortization" refer to in the context of a mortgage?

A. The process of increasing property value over time

B. The process of paying off a loan over time through regular payments

C. The process of refinancing a loan to get a lower interest rate

D. The process of selling a property before the mortgage term ends

Answer: B

Amortization refers to the process of paying off a loan over time through regular payments. Each payment is divided into principal and interest components.

➧44. What is the "debt service coverage ratio" (DSCR)?

A. Net Operating Income / Total Debt Service

B. Total Debt Service / Net Operating Income

C. Monthly Rent / Monthly Mortgage Payment

D. Monthly Mortgage Payment / Monthly Rent

Answer: A

The Debt Service Coverage Ratio (DSCR) is calculated by dividing the Net Operating Income by the Total Debt Service. It measures the property's ability to cover its debt obligations.

➡ **45. What is "net operating income" (NOI)?**

    A. Gross income minus operating expenses

    B. Gross income plus operating expenses

    C. Operating expenses minus gross income

    D. Operating expenses plus gross income

Answer: A

Net Operating Income (NOI) is the gross income generated by a property minus the operating expenses. It is a key metric for evaluating the profitability of an investment property.

➡ **46. What is "escrow" in a real estate transaction?**

    A. A legal arrangement where a third party holds funds or documents

    B. A mandatory insurance policy for the property

    C. A penalty fee for late mortgage payments

    D. A tax levied on the sale of the property

Answer: A

Escrow is a legal arrangement where a neutral third party holds funds or documents until the conditions of a contract are met. It ensures that both parties meet their obligations before the transaction is finalized..

➡ **47. What is "due diligence" in real estate?**

A. The process of verifying all aspects of a property before purchase

B. The process of securing financing for a property

C. The process of transferring property ownership

D. The process of appraising a property's value

Answer: A

Due diligence refers to the process of thoroughly investigating and verifying all aspects of a property before completing the purchase.

➠48. What is a "seller's market"?

A. A market where supply exceeds demand

B. A market where demand exceeds supply

C. A market with high interest rates

D. A market with low interest rates

Answer: B

A seller's market is characterized by high demand and low supply, often leading to higher property prices and favorable conditions for sellers.

➠49. What is "redlining"?

A. The practice of refusing loans or insurance to people based on their location

B. The practice of setting higher interest rates for riskier borrowers

C. The practice of requiring a larger down payment for expensive properties

D. The practice of conducting a detailed property inspection

Answer: A

Redlining is the discriminatory practice of refusing loans or insurance to individuals based on their geographical location, often targeting areas with a high minority population.

➠50. What is "house hacking"?

A. The practice of buying a property to rent out part of it while living in another part

B. The practice of flipping houses for profit

C. The practice of illegally occupying a vacant property

D. The practice of investing in multiple properties to diversify risk

Answer: A

House hacking refers to the practice of buying a property and living in one part of it while renting out another part to generate income.

Financing

Financing is not just a step in the process of acquiring a property; it's a journey that starts long before you even look at a home or an investment property. It's a journey that involves understanding your financial health, the market conditions, and the various financing options available to you. This chapter aims to be your comprehensive guide through this journey, covering everything from the types of loans available to the intricacies of the mortgage approval process.

Understanding Your Financial Health

Before you even consider taking out a loan, it's crucial to understand your financial health. This involves:

Credit Score

Your credit score is a numerical representation of your creditworthiness, which lenders use to gauge the risk of lending to you.

Debt-to-Income Ratio

This ratio compares your total monthly debts to your monthly income, giving lenders an idea of how much additional debt you can handle.

Savings

The amount you have saved can directly affect your down payment, affecting the types of loans you may be eligible for.

Types of Financing Options

- Conventional Loans

Conventional loans are offered by private lenders and usually require a 20% down payment. These loans are best for those with strong credit scores.

- Fixed-Rate vs. Variable-Rate

Fixed-rate loans offer a constant interest rate, while variable-rate loans fluctuate over time.

- Government-Backed Loans

FHA Loans

These loans are backed by the Federal Housing Administration and are ideal for first-time homebuyers.

VA Loans

These loans are for veterans and come with benefits like zero down payment.

USDA Loans

These are for rural property buyers and offer 100% financing.

- Specialty Loans

Bridge Loans

These are short-term loans that bridge the gap between the selling price of a new home and a homebuyer's new mortgage.

Balloon Mortgages

These have lower initial payments but require a large lump-sum payment at the end of the term.

The Role of Lenders

Lenders are not just institutions that loan you money; they are partners in your real estate journey.

- Traditional Banks

These institutions offer a variety of loan products but often have stringent criteria.

- Credit Unions

Owned by members, they often offer lower interest rates but you need to be a member to avail loans.

- Online Lenders

These offer quick approvals but may have hidden fees.

- Private Lenders

These are individuals or private companies that offer loans, often at higher interest rates.

Mortgage Approval Process

- Pre-Approval

This is an initial review of your financial health to give you an idea of the loan amount you might be approved for.

- Application & Documentation

This involves submitting various documents like tax returns, pay stubs, and bank statements.

- Appraisal

The lender will require an appraisal of the property to ensure it's worth the loan amount.

- Underwriting

This is where the lender assesses the risk of lending to you.

- Closing

This is the final step where all the legal documents are signed, and the loan is disbursed.

Risks and Mitigations

- Default Risk

This is the risk that you may not be able to repay the loan. To mitigate this, always have a financial buffer.

- Interest Rate Risk

The risk that interest rates will rise, increasing your repayment amount. Fixed-rate mortgages can mitigate this.

- Prepayment Risk

The risk that you'll be penalized for paying off the loan early. Always read the loan agreement carefully for any prepayment penalties.

Conclusion

Understanding the intricacies of real estate financing is crucial for anyone looking to buy a property. From assessing your financial health to understanding the types of loans and the role of various lenders, each step is crucial in making an informed decision. Always remember, the cheapest loan is not always the best, and the most expensive loan is not always the worst. It's all about finding the right fit for your financial situation.

Mock Exam Financing

➡1. What is a credit score primarily used for in the financing process?

    A. To determine the loan amount

    B. To assess the risk of lending to you

    C. To decide the loan term

    D. To calculate the down payment

Answer: B

Credit scores are used by lenders to assess the risk of lending to you. A higher score generally means lower risk for the lender.

➡2. What does the Debt-to-Income Ratio represent?

    A. Monthly debts to monthly income

    B. Annual debts to annual income

    C. Monthly debts to annual income

    D. Annual debts to monthly income

Answer: A

The Debt-to-Income Ratio compares your total monthly debts to your monthly income.

➡3. Which loan is ideal for first-time homebuyers?

    A. Conventional Loan

    B. FHA Loan

    C. VA Loan

    D. Bridge Loan

Answer: B

FHA loans are backed by the Federal Housing Administration and are generally easier to qualify for, making them ideal for first-time homebuyers.

➡4. What is a fixed-rate mortgage?

A. A loan with fluctuating interest rates

B. A loan with a constant interest rate

C. A loan with a balloon payment

D. A loan with no interest

Answer: B

A fixed-rate mortgage offers a constant interest rate throughout the loan term.

➡5. What is the primary benefit of a VA loan?

A. No down payment

B. No interest

C. No monthly payments

D. No closing costs

Answer: A

VA loans often require no down payment, making them beneficial for veterans.

➡6. What is the role of an underwriter in the mortgage approval process?

A. To assess the risk of lending to you

B. To appraise the property

C. To prepare legal documents

D. To sell the loan to investors

Answer: A

The underwriter assesses the risk of lending to you based on your financial health and the property's value.

➠7. What is a balloon mortgage?

    A. A loan with no interest
    B. A loan with a large lump-sum payment at the end
    C. A loan with fluctuating interest rates
    D. A loan with no down payment

Answer: B

A balloon mortgage has lower initial payments but requires a large lump-sum payment at the end of the term.

➠8. What is the primary risk of a variable-rate mortgage?

    A. Default risk
    B. Interest rate risk
    C. Prepayment risk
    D. Inflation risk

Answer: B

The primary risk of a variable-rate mortgage is that the interest rate can fluctuate, affecting your monthly payments.

➠9. What does pre-approval in the mortgage process mean?

    A. Final loan approval
    B. Initial review of your financial health
    C. Property appraisal
    D. Loan disbursal

Answer: B

Pre-approval is an initial review of your financial health to give you an idea of the loan amount you might be approved for.

➟10. What is the primary benefit of a loan from a credit union?

    A. Quick approval

    B. Lower interest rates

    C. No down payment

    D. No need for a good credit score

Answer: B

Credit unions often offer lower interest rates compared to traditional banks, but you need to be a member to avail loans.

➟11. What does LTV stand for in mortgage financing?

    A. Loan To Vendor

    B. Loan To Value

    C. Long Term Validation

    D. Loan Term Variation

Answer: B

LTV stands for Loan To Value, which is the ratio of the loan amount to the value of the property.

➟12. What is the main purpose of mortgage insurance?

    A. To protect the lender

    B. To protect the borrower

    C. To protect the property

    D. To protect the co-signer

Answer: A

Mortgage insurance is primarily designed to protect the lender in case the borrower defaults on the loan.

➡13. What is a home equity line of credit (HELOC)?

    A. A one-time loan

    B. A revolving line of credit

    C. A fixed-rate loan

    D. A government-backed loan

Answer: B

A HELOC is a revolving line of credit that allows you to borrow against the equity in your home.

➡14. What is the main disadvantage of an interest-only loan?

    A. High down payment

    B. High interest rates

    C. No equity build-up

    D. Short loan term

Answer: C

The main disadvantage of an interest-only loan is that you do not build equity since you are only paying the interest.

➡15. What is a reverse mortgage?

    A. A loan for young homebuyers

    B. A loan where the lender pays the borrower

    C. A loan with fluctuating interest rates

    D. A loan for investment properties

Answer: B

In a reverse mortgage, the lender pays the borrower, usually a senior citizen, against the home's equity.

➡16. What is the main advantage of a 15-year mortgage over a 30-year mortgage?

    A. Lower interest rates

    B. Lower monthly payments

    C. No down payment

    D. No closing costs

Answer: A

A 15-year mortgage generally offers lower interest rates compared to a 30-year mortgage.

➡17. What does APR stand for?

    A. Annual Property Rate

    B. Annual Percentage Rate

    C. Approved Payment Rate

    D. Average Payment Rate

Answer: B

APR stands for Annual Percentage Rate, which includes the interest rate and other loan costs.

➡18. What is a jumbo loan?

    A. A small loan

    B. A loan exceeding conforming loan limits

    C. A government-backed loan

    D. A loan for commercial properties

Answer: B

A jumbo loan is a loan that exceeds the conforming loan limits set by Fannie Mae and Freddie Mac.

➡19. What is the main disadvantage of a hard money loan?

A. Long loan term

B. High interest rates

C. Low loan amount

D. Strict eligibility criteria

Answer: B

The main disadvantage of a hard money loan is its high interest rates.

➡20. What is a conforming loan?

A. A loan that exceeds Fannie Mae and Freddie Mac limits

B. A loan that meets Fannie Mae and Freddie Mac guidelines

C. A government-backed loan

D. A loan for investment properties

Answer: B

A conforming loan is one that meets the guidelines set by Fannie Mae and Freddie Mac.

➡21. What is a balloon payment?

A. A small monthly payment

B. A large final payment

C. A down payment

D. An interest-only payment

Answer: B

A balloon payment is a large final payment at the end of a loan term, often after making smaller monthly payments.

➡ 22. What is a debt-to-income ratio?

A. The ratio of monthly debt payments to monthly income

B. The ratio of loan amount to property value

C. The ratio of interest rate to loan amount

D. The ratio of down payment to loan amount

Answer: A

The debt-to-income ratio is the ratio of your monthly debt payments to your monthly income, used to assess loan eligibility.

➡ 23. What does PMI stand for?

A. Property Mortgage Insurance

B. Private Mortgage Insurance

C. Public Mortgage Investment

D. Personal Monthly Installment

Answer: B

PMI stands for Private Mortgage Insurance, which protects the lender in case of borrower default.

➡ 24. What is the primary purpose of a rate lock in mortgage financing?

A. To increase the interest rate over time

B. To decrease the interest rate over time

C. To secure an interest rate for a specified period

D. To allow fluctuation of the interest rate

Answer: C

The primary purpose of a rate lock is to secure a specific interest rate for a specified period, protecting the borrower from rate fluctuations during that time.

➡ 25. What is an escrow account primarily used for?

    A. Investing in stocks

    B. Paying off the loan early

    C. Holding funds for property taxes and insurance

    D. Saving for a down payment

Answer: C

An escrow account is primarily used to hold funds for property taxes and insurance.

➡ 26. What is a subprime mortgage?

    A. A mortgage for high-credit borrowers

    B. A mortgage for low-credit borrowers

    C. A government-backed mortgage

    D. A mortgage for investment properties

Answer: B

A subprime mortgage is designed for borrowers with low credit scores.

➡ 27. What is a VA loan?

    A. A loan for veterans

    B. A loan for vacation homes

    C. A loan for variable assets

    D. A loan for very affluent individuals

Answer: A

A VA loan is a mortgage loan for veterans, backed by the Department of Veterans Affairs.

➡28. What is a pre-approval letter?

    A. A letter confirming loan denial

    B. A letter confirming loan approval

    C. A letter estimating how much you can borrow

    D. A letter confirming property value

Answer: C

A pre-approval letter is an estimate from a lender indicating how much you may be able to borrow.

➡29. What is a bridge loan?

    A. A long-term loan

    B. A short-term loan

    C. A loan for construction projects

    D. A loan for first-time homebuyers

Answer: B

A bridge loan is a short-term loan used until a person secures permanent financing.

➡30. What is a credit score primarily used for in mortgage financing?

    A. To determine loan eligibility

    B. To determine property value

    C. To determine loan term

    D. To determine down payment amount

Answer: A

A credit score is primarily used to determine loan eligibility and interest rates.

➡ 31. What is the Debt-to-Income (DTI) ratio primarily used for?

    A. To determine the borrower's credit score

    B. To evaluate the borrower's ability to repay the loan

    C. To calculate the property tax

    D. To assess the value of the property

Answer: B

The Debt-to-Income ratio is used to evaluate a borrower's ability to repay the loan by comparing their debt payments to their income.

➡ 32. What does APR stand for in the context of mortgage loans?

    A. Annual Property Rate

    B. Average Payment Rate

    C. Annual Percentage Rate

    D. Approved Payment Rate

Answer: C

APR stands for Annual Percentage Rate, which includes the interest rate and other loan costs, providing a more complete picture of the loan's cost.

➡ 33. What is the primary purpose of a loan origination fee?

    A. To cover the cost of property appraisal

    B. To compensate the lender for processing the loan

    C. To pay for the borrower's credit report

    D. To fund the escrow account

Answer: B

The loan origination fee is primarily charged to compensate the lender for the cost of processing the loan.

➡34. What does a mortgage refinance involve?

   A. Changing the terms of your existing mortgage

   B. Transferring your mortgage to another lender

   C. Converting an ARM to a fixed-rate mortgage

   D. Paying off the mortgage early

Answer: A

A mortgage refinance involves changing the terms of your existing mortgage, often to take advantage of lower interest rates.

➡35. What is the Debt-to-Income (DTI) ratio used for in mortgage financing?

   A. To determine the borrower's credit score

   B. To assess the borrower's ability to repay the loan

   C. To calculate the loan-to-value ratio

   D. To set the interest rate on the loan

Answer: B

The Debt-to-Income (DTI) ratio is used to assess a borrower's ability to repay the loan. It compares the borrower's total monthly debt payments to their gross monthly income.

➡36. What is a pre-approval letter in the context of mortgage financing?

   A. A letter confirming the property's appraisal value

   B. A letter from the lender indicating a borrower's eligibility for a loan

   C. A letter confirming the loan has been fully paid off

   D. A letter from the borrower to the lender requesting loan modification

Answer: B

A pre-approval letter is issued by a lender and indicates that the borrower has been reviewed and is eligible for a loan up to a certain amount.

37. What is the primary purpose of private mortgage insurance (PMI)?

A. To protect the borrower from foreclosure

B. To protect the lender in case of borrower default

C. To lower the interest rate

D. To eliminate the need for a down payment

Answer: B

Private Mortgage Insurance (PMI) is designed to protect the lender in case the borrower defaults on the loan.

38. What does underwriting involve in mortgage financing?

A. Property appraisal

B. Loan approval process

C. Monthly payment calculation

D. Closing the loan

Answer: B

Underwriting involves the process of evaluating the risk of insuring the mortgage, effectively approving or denying the loan.

39. What is the main disadvantage of an adjustable-rate mortgage (ARM)?

A. High down payment

B. Fluctuating interest rates

C. High closing costs

D. Fixed interest rate

Answer: B

The main disadvantage of an adjustable-rate mortgage is that the interest rate can fluctuate, potentially increasing the borrower's monthly payments.

➡40. What is the primary purpose of a "balloon payment" in a mortgage?

A. To reduce the monthly mortgage payments

B. To pay off the mortgage early

C. To adjust the interest rate

D. To refinance the mortgage

Answer: A

The primary purpose of a "balloon payment" is to reduce the monthly mortgage payments for a set period. At the end of that period, the remaining balance is due in a lump sum, known as the "balloon payment."

➡41. What is the main advantage of a fixed-rate mortgage over an adjustable-rate mortgage?

A. Lower initial interest rates

B. Interest rates can decrease over time

C. Interest rate remains constant

D. Easier to qualify for

Answer: C

The main advantage of a fixed-rate mortgage is that the interest rate remains constant throughout the loan term, providing stability in monthly payments.

➡42. What is the Loan-to-Value (LTV) ratio?

A. The ratio of the loan amount to the appraised value of the property

B. The ratio of the loan amount to the selling price of the property

C. The ratio of the down payment to the loan amount

D. The ratio of the interest rate to the loan amount

Answer: A

The Loan-to-Value (LTV) ratio is the ratio of the loan amount to the appraised value of the property. It is used to assess risk by lenders.

➡️43. What does a "due-on-sale" clause in a mortgage contract mean?

    A. The entire loan amount is due if the property is sold

    B. Monthly payments are due on the date of sale

    C. The loan can be assumed by the buyer

    D. The interest rate will increase upon sale

Answer: A

A "due-on-sale" clause means that the entire loan amount becomes due if the property is sold. This prevents the new buyer from assuming the existing mortgage.

➡️44. What is a "subprime" mortgage?

    A. A mortgage for high-income borrowers

    B. A mortgage with below-average interest rates

    C. A mortgage for borrowers with poor credit history

    D. A mortgage that is secondary to the primary loan

Answer: C

A "subprime" mortgage is designed for borrowers with poor credit history and usually comes with higher interest rates to compensate for the increased risk to the lender.

➡️45. What is the purpose of Private Mortgage Insurance (PMI)?

    A. To protect the lender if the borrower defaults

    B. To protect the borrower from high interest rates

    C. To provide tax benefits to the borrower

    D. To allow the borrower to make smaller down payments

Answer: A

The purpose of Private Mortgage Insurance (PMI) is to protect the lender in case the borrower defaults on the loan. It is usually required when the down payment is less than 20%.

➡️46. What is the primary function of a mortgage broker?

    A. To lend money directly to borrowers

    B. To connect borrowers with suitable lenders

    C. To appraise the value of the property

    D. To manage the property after purchase

Answer: B

The primary function of a mortgage broker is to connect borrowers with suitable lenders. They do not lend money directly but act as intermediaries.

➡️47. What does the term "underwriting" refer to in the context of mortgage financing?

    A. The process of evaluating the risk of lending to a borrower

    B. The process of appraising the property value

    C. The process of setting the interest rate

    D. The process of collecting monthly payments

Answer: A

Underwriting refers to the process of evaluating the risk of lending to a borrower. It involves assessing creditworthiness, income, and other factors.

➡️48. What is a "prepayment penalty"?

    A. A fee for making larger-than-required payments

    B. A fee for refinancing the mortgage

C. A fee for paying off the loan early

D. A fee for late payments

Answer: C

A prepayment penalty is a fee charged by some lenders for paying off the loan before the end of its term. This is to compensate for the interest the lender will lose.

➡**49. What does "loan-to-value ratio" (LTV) indicate?**

A. The ratio of the loan amount to the borrower's income

B. The ratio of the loan amount to the appraised value of the property

C. The ratio of the interest rate to the loan amount

D. The ratio of the down payment to the loan amount

Answer: B

The loan-to-value ratio (LTV) indicates the ratio of the loan amount to the appraised value of the property. It is a measure used by lenders to assess risk.

➡**50. What does "escrow" refer to in the context of mortgage financing?**

A. A legal agreement between buyer and seller

B. A separate account for taxes and insurance

C. A penalty for early loan repayment

D. An adjustable interest rate

Answer: B

In the context of mortgage financing, escrow refers to a separate account where funds for property taxes and insurance are held until they are due.

Transfer of Property

The transfer of property is not just a transaction; it's a complex legal process that requires meticulous attention to detail. Whether you're a first-time homebuyer, a seasoned investor, or a professional in the real estate industry, understanding the nuances of property transfer is crucial. This chapter will serve as an exhaustive guide, covering everything from the types of property transfers to the legal and financial intricacies involved.

Types of Property Transfers

Simple Sale

In a simple sale, the buyer and seller agree on a price, usually after some negotiation. But what seems straightforward is often not. The sale is subject to various conditions such as inspections, appraisals, and loan approvals. Each of these steps can present challenges that need to be navigated carefully.

Gift

Transferring property as a gift may seem simple but can be fraught with complications, including potential tax liabilities. The IRS has specific guidelines about gift taxes and exemptions, which must be carefully considered.

Inheritance

Inheritance laws vary by state and can be complicated by the presence of a will, or lack thereof. The probate process can be long and arduous, involving not just legal but also emotional considerations.

Foreclosure

Foreclosure is a legal process where a lender attempts to recover the balance of a loan from a borrower who has stopped making payments. This process varies by state and can be incredibly complex, involving multiple legal and financial steps.

Eminent Domain

This is a legal strategy that allows a government to acquire private property for public use. However, the Fifth Amendment to the U.S. Constitution requires "just compensation," the specifics of which can be a matter of intense negotiation or even litigation.

Legal Instruments for Property Transfer

General Warranty Deed

This type of deed offers the most comprehensive protection to the buyer. It guarantees that the property is free from all encumbrances, whether they are known or unknown. This is often the preferred deed for buyers but may require additional legal work to prepare.

Special Warranty Deed

This deed is more limited in scope, offering guarantees only against encumbrances or claims that occurred during the time the seller owned the property. This is often used in commercial real estate transactions.

Quitclaim Deed

This deed transfers whatever ownership the seller has, making no guarantees. It's often used between family members or to clear up a title, but it's risky for buyers because there are no guarantees.

Due Diligence

Title Search

A title search is not just a formality; it's a crucial step in protecting your investment. This search will reveal if there are any liens, easements, or other encumbrances on the property.

Home Inspection

A home inspection can reveal hidden issues with a property that could affect its value or livability. From structural issues to plumbing and electrical systems, a thorough inspection can save you from costly mistakes.

Appraisal

An appraisal is not just about confirming the sale price; it's also a requirement for most mortgage lenders. The appraiser will evaluate the property based on various factors, including comparable sales, to arrive at a market value.

Financial Aspects

Down Payment

The down payment is often the biggest financial hurdle in a property transfer. It's not just about having the money; it's also about proving to lenders that you're a low-risk borrower.

Closing Costs

These costs can include a range of fees, from attorney's fees to title insurance, and can add up to a significant amount. Understanding these costs in advance can help you budget more accurately.

Financing

Financing options are numerous, from traditional fixed-rate mortgages to adjustable-rate mortgages (ARMs) and interest-only loans. Each has its pros and cons, and understanding these can save you money in the long run.

Taxes and Fees

Stamp Duty

Also known as transfer tax, stamp duty can be a significant cost in some states. It's usually a percentage of the property's value and is paid at closing.

Capital Gains Tax

If you're selling a property that has appreciated in value, you may be subject to capital gains tax. However, there are exemptions and strategies to minimize this tax.

Property Tax

Property taxes are an ongoing cost that can vary widely by location. They're usually paid semi-annually or annually and are subject to change based on local tax assessments.

Legal Requirements and Procedures

Contract of Sale

This is the foundational document for any property transfer. It outlines every aspect of the transaction, from the sale price to the closing date, and any contingencies that must be met.

Escrow

An escrow service acts as a neutral third party to hold funds and documents until all conditions are met. It's a layer of protection for both buyer and seller.

Closing

Closing is the final step, but it involves numerous sub-steps, including a final walkthrough, signing of documents, and the actual transfer of funds. Each of these requires careful attention to detail.

Conclusion

The transfer of property is a multifaceted process that involves a range of legal, financial, and procedural steps. Whether you're a buyer or a seller, understanding these elements deeply can not only facilitate a smoother transaction but also potentially save you thousands of dollars and legal headaches. This chapter has aimed to be your comprehensive guide to understanding all the aspects involved in the transfer of property.

Mock Exam Transfer of Property

➡1. **What is the primary purpose of a title search?**

A. To find the original owner

B. To check for any liens or encumbrances

C. To determine the property's market value

D. To inspect the property's condition

Answer: B

The primary purpose of a title search is to check for any liens, easements, or other encumbrances on the property.

➡2. **Which type of deed offers the most comprehensive protection to the buyer?**

A. Quitclaim Deed

B. Special Warranty Deed

C. General Warranty Deed

D. Bargain and Sale Deed

Answer: C

A General Warranty Deed offers the most comprehensive protection to the buyer, guaranteeing that the property is free from all encumbrances.

➡3. **What is the role of an escrow service?**

A. To provide financing

B. To act as a neutral third party

C. To perform a home inspection

D. To appraise the property

Answer: B

An escrow service acts as a neutral third party to hold funds and documents until all conditions are met.

➡ 4. What does the Contract of Sale outline?

    A. The buyer's financing options

    B. The seller's capital gains tax

    C. Every aspect of the transaction

    D. The buyer's down payment amount

Answer: C

The Contract of Sale outlines every aspect of the transaction, from the sale price to the closing date and any contingencies.

➡ 5. Which of the following is NOT a type of property transfer?

    A. Simple Sale

    B. Gift

    C. Inheritance

    D. Mortgage

Answer: D

Mortgage is not a type of property transfer; it is a type of financing.

➡ 6. What is the primary purpose of a home inspection?

    A. To appraise the property

    B. To reveal hidden issues

    C. To fulfill legal requirements

    D. To negotiate the sale price

Answer: B

The primary purpose of a home inspection is to reveal any hidden issues with the property that could affect its value or livability.

➡7. **What is stamp duty?**

A. A type of property tax

B. A type of income tax

C. A type of transfer tax

D. A type of sales tax

Answer: C

Stamp duty, also known as transfer tax, is usually a percentage of the property's value and is paid at closing.

➡8. **Which of the following is a financial aspect of property transfer?**

A. Title search

B. Down payment

C. Home inspection

D. General Warranty Deed

Answer: B

The down payment is a financial aspect of property transfer and is often the biggest financial hurdle in a property transfer.

➡9. **What does the Fifth Amendment to the U.S. Constitution require in cases of eminent domain?**

A. Just compensation

B. Prior notice

C. A jury trial

D. Consent of the owner

Answer: A

The Fifth Amendment requires "just compensation" in cases where the government acquires private property for public use.

→10. What is the risk associated with a Quitclaim Deed?

    A. High cost

    B. Time-consuming process

    C. No guarantees

    D. Legal complications

Answer: C

A Quitclaim Deed transfers whatever ownership the seller has, making no guarantees. It's often used between family members or to clear up a title but is risky for buyers.

→11. What is the role of a title company in a property transfer?

    A. To provide financing

    B. To act as a mediator

    C. To ensure the title is clear

    D. To appraise the property

Answer: C

The title company ensures that the title to a piece of real estate is legitimate and then issues title insurance for that property.

→12. What is the primary purpose of a deed?

    A. To outline the terms of a mortgage

    B. To transfer ownership of property

    C. To list property defects

    D. To describe the property boundaries

Answer: B

The primary purpose of a deed is to transfer ownership from the seller to the buyer.

➡13. What does "chain of title" refer to?

   A. A series of owners of a property

   B. The legal description of a property

   C. The financing options for a property

   D. The zoning laws affecting a property

Answer: A

The "chain of title" refers to the complete unbroken ownership record of a property, tracing it back to the original owner.

➡14. What is a "1031 exchange"?

   A. A type of mortgage

   B. A tax-deferred property exchange

   C. A type of property insurance

   D. A type of property appraisal

Answer: B

A "1031 exchange" allows the owner to sell a property and reinvest the proceeds in a new property while deferring all capital gain taxes.

➡15. What is the purpose of a "closing statement"?

   A. To finalize the sale

   B. To initiate the sale

   C. To list property defects

   D. To describe the property boundaries

Answer: A

The closing statement, also known as a HUD-1, finalizes the sale and outlines all costs for both the buyer and the seller.

➡16. What is "adverse possession"?

A. Illegal occupation of a property

B. A type of property insurance

C. Gaining legal ownership through extended occupation

D. A type of property tax

Answer: C

Adverse possession allows someone to gain legal ownership of a property after occupying it for an extended period, provided certain conditions are met.

➡17. What is the "right of first refusal"?

A. The right to reject a property

B. The right to be the first to purchase a property

C. The right to a home inspection

D. The right to back out of a sale

Answer: B

The "right of first refusal" gives someone the opportunity to be the first to purchase a property before the owner sells it to someone else.

➡18. What is a "land contract"?

A. A rental agreement

B. A type of mortgage

C. A seller financing option

D. A property appraisal

Answer: C

A land contract is a seller financing option where the buyer makes payments to the seller instead of a traditional mortgage lender.

➡ **19. What is "escrow"?**

   A. A type of deed

   B. A neutral third party in a transaction

   C. A type of property insurance

   D. A legal description of a property

Answer: B

Escrow refers to a neutral third party that holds funds or documents until the conditions of a contract are met.

➡ **20. What is a "purchase agreement"?**

   A. A formal offer to buy a property

   B. A type of property insurance

   C. A legal description of a property

   D. A type of mortgage

Answer: A

A purchase agreement is a formal offer to buy a property and outlines the terms and conditions of the sale.

➡ **21. What does "encumbrance" refer to in real estate?**

   A. A type of property insurance

   B. A claim against a property

   C. The legal description of a property

   D. A type of mortgage

Answer: B

An encumbrance is a claim against a property, such as a lien or mortgage, that may diminish its value or impede its sale.

➡22. What is "equity" in the context of property ownership?

    A. The market value of a property

    B. The difference between the property's value and the mortgage balance

    C. A type of property insurance

    D. A legal claim against a property

Answer: B

Equity is the difference between the market value of the property and the remaining balance on any mortgages or loans against the property.

➡23. What is a "quitclaim deed"?

    A. A deed that transfers ownership with warranties

    B. A deed that transfers ownership without warranties

    C. A legal description of a property

    D. A type of property insurance

Answer: B

A quitclaim deed transfers ownership without any warranties, meaning the seller does not guarantee that they own the property free and clear.

➡24. What is "amortization"?

    A. The process of increasing property value

    B. The process of paying off debt in regular installments

    C. A type of property insurance

    D. A legal claim against a property

Answer: B

Amortization is the process of paying off a debt, such as a mortgage, in regular installments over a period of time.

➡**25. What does "underwriting" refer to in the context of property financing?**

    A. Assessing the risk of lending to a borrower

    B. The legal description of a property

    C. A type of property insurance

    D. A legal claim against a property

Answer: A

Underwriting refers to the process where a lender assesses the risk of lending to a particular borrower, often determining the terms of the loan.

➡**26. What does "right of first refusal" mean in a real estate context?**

    A. The right to refuse a property inspection

    B. The right to purchase a property before the owner sells it to someone else

    C. The right to refuse to pay property taxes

    D. The right to refuse to make mortgage payments

Answer: B

The right of first refusal is a contractual right that gives its holder the option to enter a business transaction with the owner of something, according to specified terms, before the owner is entitled to enter into that transaction with a third party.

➡**27. What is a "balloon payment"?**

    A. A small monthly payment

    B. A large final payment at the end of a loan term

    C. A down payment

D. An insurance premium

Answer: B

A balloon payment is a large, lump-sum payment that is due at the end of some mortgage contracts or other term loans.

➡28. What is "redlining"?

   A. A type of home inspection

   B. Discriminatory practice of refusing loans in certain neighborhoods

   C. A method of property valuation

   D. A type of mortgage

Answer: B

Redlining is the discriminatory practice where financial institutions refuse to lend money or extend credit to borrowers in certain areas of town, often based on the racial or ethnic composition of those areas.

➡29. What does "underwater" mean in terms of a mortgage?

   A. The mortgage is in good standing

   B. The mortgage is paid off

   C. The value of the property is less than the remaining mortgage balance

   D. The mortgage has a low interest rate

Answer: C

Being "underwater" on a mortgage means that the value of the property is less than the amount remaining on the mortgage, often leading to negative equity.

➡30. What is "leverage" in real estate?

   A. Using borrowed funds for investment

B. A type of mortgage

C. A legal claim against a property

D. A type of property insurance

Answer: A

Leverage in real estate refers to using borrowed funds to finance the purchase of a property, aiming to earn a return greater than the interest payable.

➠31. What is a "lien"?

A. A legal claim against a property

B. A type of mortgage

C. A legal description of a property

D. A type of property insurance

Answer: A

A lien is a legal claim against a property, usually as security for a debt or obligation.

➠32. What is "market value"?

A. The price a property is listed for

B. The price a property would sell for in a competitive market

C. A type of mortgage

D. A legal claim against a property

Answer: B

Market value is the price at which a property would sell in a competitive and open market, assuming both buyer and seller are knowledgeable and willing.

➠33. What is "negative amortization"?

A. When the loan balance decreases

B. When the loan balance increases

C. A type of mortgage

D. A legal claim against a property

Answer: B

Negative amortization occurs when the monthly payments are not enough to cover the interest costs, resulting in an increasing loan balance.

➠34. What is "origination fee"?

A. A fee for property appraisal

B. A fee charged by a lender to process a new loan

C. A type of mortgage

D. A legal claim against a property

Answer: B

An origination fee is a charge by the lender for processing a new loan, often expressed as a percentage of the loan amount.

➠35. What is "pre-qualification"?

A. A preliminary assessment of a borrower's ability to secure a loan

B. A type of mortgage

C. A legal claim against a property

D. A type of property insurance

Answer: A

Pre-qualification is a lender's preliminary assessment of a borrower's ability to secure a loan, usually before the borrower makes an offer on a property.

➠36. What is the role of a "warranty deed" in a property transfer?

A. It guarantees that the property is free from liens

B. It transfers only the ownership rights the grantor has

C. It is used in foreclosure sales

D. It transfers property to a trust

Answer: A

A warranty deed guarantees that the property is free from liens or other encumbrances, except those listed in the deed.

➡️**37. What does "cloud on title" mean?**

A. A pending lawsuit affecting ownership

B. A clear ownership history

C. A mortgage approval

D. A property inspection

Answer: A

A cloud on title refers to any outstanding claim or encumbrance that could impair the title.

➡️**38. What is "eminent domain"?**

A. The right of the government to acquire private property for public use

B. The right of a tenant to purchase the property

C. The right of a bank to seize property for unpaid mortgage

D. The right of a property owner to change zoning laws

Answer: A

Eminent domain is the right of a government to acquire private property for public use, with compensation.

➡️**39. What is "abstract of title"?**

A. A summary of the legal history of a piece of property

B. A legal description of the property

C. A list of previous owners

D. A list of property restrictions

Answer: A

An abstract of title is a summary of the legal history of a piece of property, including ownership and encumbrances.

➡ **40. What is "tenancy in common"?**

A. A form of property ownership where two or more people own property together

B. A form of property ownership where property is owned by a single individual

C. A form of property ownership where property is owned by a married couple

D. A form of property ownership where property is owned by a corporation

Answer: A

Tenancy in common is a form of ownership where two or more people have an undivided interest in property, without the right of survivorship.

➡ **41. What is a "deed in lieu of foreclosure"?**

A. A deed used to transfer property back to the lender to avoid foreclosure

B. A deed that transfers property to a new owner

C. A deed that includes warranties against liens

D. A deed used in auction sales

Answer: A

A deed in lieu of foreclosure is a deed instrument in which a mortgagor conveys all interest in a real property to the mortgagee to satisfy a loan that is in default and avoid foreclosure proceedings.

➡️**42. What does "chain of title" refer to?**

    A. The sequence of historical transfers of title to a property

    B. The list of all tenants who have occupied a property

    C. The chronological order of construction permits for a property

    D. The list of all financial transactions related to a property

Answer: A

The chain of title refers to the sequence of historical transfers of title to a property. It is crucial for determining the current legal owner and any encumbrances or liens on the property.

➡️**43. What does "chain of title" refer to?**

    A. A series of owners of a particular property

    B. The process of mortgage approval

    C. A type of property insurance

    D. A method of property valuation

Answer: A

The chain of title refers to the complete unbroken ownership history of a property.

➡️**44. What is a "balloon payment"?**

    A. A small monthly payment

    B. A large final payment at the end of a loan term

    C. A payment made annually

    D. A payment made to remove a lien

Answer: B

A balloon payment is a large, lump-sum payment scheduled at the end of a series of smaller periodic payments.

➡45. What is "equity" in terms of real estate?

A. The difference between the property's market value and the remaining mortgage balance

B. The initial down payment

C. The interest rate on a mortgage

D. The monthly mortgage payment

Answer: A

Equity is the difference between the market value of the property and the amount still owed on its mortgage.

➡46. What is "escrow"?

A. A type of mortgage

B. A legal document transferring property

C. A neutral third party that holds funds or documents until conditions are met

D. A method of property valuation

Answer: C

Escrow is a financial arrangement where a third party holds and regulates payment of the funds required for two parties involved in a given transaction.

➡47. What is a "contingency" in a real estate contract?

A. A penalty for late payment

B. A condition that must be met for the contract to be binding

C. A fixed interest rate

D. A type of property insurance

Answer: B

A contingency is a condition or action that must be met for a real estate contract to become binding.

➡48. What does "amortization" mean in a mortgage context?

    A. The process of increasing property value

    B. The process of paying off debt with a fixed repayment schedule

    C. The act of transferring property

    D. The process of dividing a large payment into smaller payments

Answer: B

Amortization is the process of paying off a debt, such as a mortgage, over time in regular installments.

➡49. What is the significance of a "quitclaim deed"?

    A. It transfers all of the grantor's interest in the property

    B. It guarantees that the property is free from liens

    C. It transfers only the ownership rights the grantor has, without any warranties

    D. It is used to transfer property to a trust

Answer: C

A quitclaim deed transfers only the ownership rights the grantor has, without any warranties or guarantees. It is often used to clear up title issues.

➡50. What is the primary purpose of a "warranty deed"?

    A. To transfer ownership without any guarantees

    B. To confirm that the grantor owns the property and it is free from liens

    C. To transfer property to a trust

    D. To serve as a temporary transfer of ownership

Answer: B

A warranty deed is used to transfer property ownership and provides the strongest protection for the buyer. It confirms that the grantor owns the property and that it is free from liens or other encumbrances.

Practice of Real Estate and Disclosures

The practice of real estate is not just about buying and selling properties; it's a multifaceted discipline that involves a deep understanding of market dynamics, legal frameworks, and ethical considerations. One of the most critical aspects of real estate practice is the concept of disclosures. This chapter aims to provide a comprehensive guide to the intricacies of real estate practice, with a particular focus on the legal and ethical requirements surrounding disclosures.

The Role of a Real Estate Agent

- Responsibilities

Real estate agents have a plethora of responsibilities, including but not limited to, listing properties, conducting market analyses, negotiating contracts, and coordinating with other professionals like home inspectors, mortgage brokers, and legal advisors. They are often the first point of contact for clients and act as a liaison between various parties involved in a real estate transaction.

- Legal Obligations

Agents are bound by a set of legal obligations that govern their professional conduct. These obligations are designed to protect the interests of the client and ensure a fair and transparent transaction process.

Fiduciary Duties

Real estate agents owe fiduciary duties to their clients, which include loyalty, confidentiality, obedience, and full disclosure. These duties are not just ethical guidelines but are enshrined in law, and failure to adhere to them can result in severe legal repercussions, including fines and loss of licensure.

Types of Disclosures

Material Facts

Material facts are any facts that could influence a buyer's decision to go through with a purchase or a seller's decision to sell. These could range from structural issues with the property, such as a weak foundation, to external factors like future construction plans in the area that might affect the property's value.

Seller's Disclosure

The seller is often required by state law to provide a detailed written disclosure statement outlining the condition of the property. This statement is comprehensive and includes everything from the age of the property to any known defects or issues that could affect its value or livability.

Environmental Disclosures

In some cases, sellers are also required to disclose information about the property's environmental conditions, such as soil contamination or flood risks. Failure to disclose such information can lead to legal consequences.

Lead-Based Paint Disclosure

Federal law mandates that sellers disclose any known presence of lead-based paint for properties built before 1978. This is a critical disclosure as exposure to lead can have severe health implications.

Importance of Disclosures

Protecting Both Parties

Disclosures serve to protect both the buyer and the seller by ensuring that all parties have the most accurate and comprehensive information possible. For the buyer, disclosures reduce the risk of moving into a home only to discover costly problems. For the seller, making full disclosures protects against future legal claims from a dissatisfied buyer.

Legal Consequences of Non-Disclosure

Failure to disclose known issues can result in legal action against the seller and the listing agent. Penalties can range from fines to legal fees and even the rescinding of the property sale.

The Disclosure Process

Timing of Disclosures

The timing of disclosures is crucial. Sellers are generally required to make all disclosures before the final sale contract is signed. This allows the buyer to make an informed decision and, if necessary, negotiate the terms of the purchase.

Buyer's Due Diligence

Upon receiving the disclosures, the buyer typically has a due diligence period, during which they can conduct their own inspections and investigations. If undisclosed issues are discovered during this period, the buyer has the right to renegotiate or even withdraw from the deal without penalty.

Conclusion

The practice of real estate is a complex, legally-driven field that requires a high level of expertise and ethical conduct. Disclosures are a critical component of this practice, serving to protect both buyers and sellers from legal repercussions and ensuring a fair, transparent transaction process. By understanding and adhering to the principles of good practice and the legal requirements of disclosures, real estate professionals can maintain the integrity of the industry and provide the best possible service to their clients.

Mock Exam Practice of Real Estate and Disclosures

➡1. What is the primary role of a real estate agent?

A. Home inspector

B. Listing properties

C. Mortgage broker

D. Legal advisor

Answer: B

The primary role of a real estate agent is to list properties and act as a liaison between various parties involved in a real estate transaction.

➡2. What does the term "fiduciary duties" refer to?

A. Legal obligations

B. Ethical guidelines

C. Both A and B

D. Neither A nor B

Answer: C

Fiduciary duties refer to both legal obligations and ethical guidelines that govern the conduct of real estate agents.

➡3. What is a material fact?

A. A fact that influences the buyer's decision

B. A fact that influences the seller's decision

C. Both A and B

D. Neither A nor B

Answer: C

A material fact is any fact that could influence either the buyer's or the seller's decision in a real estate transaction.

➡4. What is the purpose of a disclosure statement?

　　A. To reveal the seller's financial status

　　B. To reveal any known defects or issues with the property

　　C. To disclose the agent's commission

　　D. To provide a history of the property's previous owners

Answer: B

The purpose of a disclosure statement is to reveal any known defects or issues with the property to potential buyers.

➡5. What is dual agency?

　　A. When an agent represents both the buyer and the seller

　　B. When two agents work for the same brokerage

　　C. When an agent represents multiple buyers

　　D. When an agent represents multiple sellers

Answer: A

Dual agency occurs when a real estate agent represents both the buyer and the seller in the same transaction.

➡6. What does the acronym RESPA stand for?

　　A. Real Estate Settlement Procedures Act

　　B. Real Estate Sales Professional Association

　　C. Residential Estate Sales and Purchase Act

D. Real Estate Service Providers Act

Answer: A

RESPA stands for Real Estate Settlement Procedures Act, which aims to provide consumers with improved disclosures of settlement costs and to eliminate abusive practices.

➡7. What is the primary purpose of a title search?

    A. To determine the property's market value

    B. To verify the legal owner of the property

    C. To assess property taxes

    D. To inspect the property's condition

Answer: B

The primary purpose of a title search is to verify the legal owner of the property and ensure that there are no liens or other encumbrances.

➡8. What is the role of an escrow officer?

    A. To inspect the property

    B. To hold and disburse funds during a transaction

    C. To negotiate the price

    D. To list the property

Answer: B

An escrow officer holds and disburses funds during a real estate transaction, ensuring that all conditions are met before the sale is finalized.

➡9. What does a Comparative Market Analysis (CMA) help to determine?

    A. The property's legal status

B. The property's market value

C. The property's zoning classification

D. The property's tax assessment

Answer: B

A Comparative Market Analysis (CMA) is used to help determine the market value of a property by comparing it to similar properties that have recently sold or are currently listed.

➡ **10. What is the main objective of a home inspection?**

A. To assess the property's market value

B. To identify any defects or issues with the property

C. To verify the property's legal status

D. To negotiate the price

Answer: B

The main objective of a home inspection is to identify any defects or issues with the property, providing the buyer with the information needed to make an informed decision.

➡ **11. What is the primary role of the Federal Housing Administration (FHA)?**

A. To provide mortgage insurance

B. To regulate real estate agents

C. To assess property taxes

D. To conduct home inspections

Answer: A

The primary role of the FHA is to provide mortgage insurance, making it easier for borrowers to qualify for home loans.

➡ **12. What is a "contingency" in a real estate contract?**

A. A mandatory fee

B. A binding agreement

C. A conditional clause

D. An illegal provision

Answer: C

A contingency is a conditional clause that must be met for the contract to be fully enforceable.

➡**13. What does "under contract" mean in real estate?**

A. The property is being inspected

B. An offer has been accepted, but the sale is not yet complete

C. The property is listed for sale

D. The property has been sold

Answer: B

"Under contract" means that an offer has been accepted, but the sale has not yet been finalized.

➡**14. What is the purpose of earnest money?**

A. To pay for the home inspection

B. To show the seller that the buyer is serious

C. To cover closing costs

D. To pay the real estate agent's commission

Answer: B

Earnest money is a deposit made to a seller to show the buyer's good faith in a transaction.

➡**15. What is a "puffing" statement?**

A. A legal description of the property

B. An exaggerated claim to promote a property

C. A factual statement about the property's condition

D. A statement made under oath

Answer: B

A "puffing" statement is an exaggerated claim made to promote a property, and it is not legally binding.

➠16. What is the primary purpose of a "walk-through" before closing?

A. To conduct a final inspection

B. To assess the property's value

C. To finalize the mortgage terms

D. To sign the closing documents

Answer: A

The primary purpose of a walk-through is to conduct a final inspection to ensure the property's condition has not changed and that agreed-upon repairs have been made.

➠17. What does "FSBO" stand for?

A. For Sale By Order

B. For Sale By Owner

C. Full Service Buyer's Offer

D. Fixed Sale By Operator

Answer: B

FSBO stands for For Sale By Owner, indicating that the property is being sold without a listing agent.

➠18. What is a "balloon payment"?

A. A small, initial down payment

B. A large, final payment at the end of a loan term

C. A monthly mortgage payment

D. An annual property tax payment

Answer: B

A balloon payment is a large, lump-sum payment that is due at the end of a loan term.

➡19. What is the role of a "listing agent"?

A. To represent the buyer

B. To represent the seller

C. To conduct the home inspection

D. To provide mortgage financing

Answer: B

The role of a listing agent is to represent the seller in a real estate transaction.

➡20. What does "amortization" refer to?

A. The process of increasing property value

B. The process of paying off a loan over time

C. The process of dividing property among heirs

D. The process of assessing property taxes

Answer: B

Amortization refers to the process of paying off a loan over time through regular payments.

➡21. What is the primary purpose of a Comparative Market Analysis (CMA)?

A. To determine the property's tax value

B. To set the rent for a property

C. To establish a listing price for a property

D. To assess the property for insurance purposes

Answer: C

A Comparative Market Analysis is primarily used to establish a reasonable listing price for a property based on similar properties in the area.

➡ **22. What does "chain of title" refer to?**

A. The sequence of historical transfers of title to a property

B. The list of previous owners

C. The legal description of the property

D. The list of recorded liens against the property

Answer: A

The chain of title refers to the sequence of historical transfers of title to a property.

➡ **23. What is the primary purpose of a "puffing" statement in real estate advertising?**

A. To provide factual information

B. To exaggerate for effect

C. To disclose all known defects

D. To mislead potential buyers

Answer: B

Puffing refers to exaggerated statements used to make a property seem more appealing. They are not considered legally binding.

➡ **24. What does "escrow" mean in real estate?**

A. A legal document

B. A neutral third party

C. A type of mortgage

D. A preliminary agreement

Answer: B

In real estate, escrow refers to a neutral third party that holds funds or documents until the transaction is completed.

➡25. What is the "right of first refusal" in a real estate context?

A. The right to be the first to view a property

B. The right to match an offer on a property before it is sold to another buyer

C. The right to refuse any offer on a property

D. The right to be the first to make an offer on a property

Answer: B

The right of first refusal allows an individual or entity the opportunity to match an offer on a property before it is sold to another buyer.

➡26. What is the purpose of a "title search"?

A. To find the property's legal description

B. To verify the legal owner of the property

C. To determine the property's market value

D. To find any restrictions on the property

Answer: B

The purpose of a title search is to verify the legal owner of the property.

➡27. What is "amortization"?

A. The process of increasing property value

B. The process of paying off a loan over time

C. The division of a large property into smaller lots

D. The depreciation of property value over time

Answer: B

Amortization is the process of paying off a loan over time through regular payments.

➡**28. What is the "due diligence" period in a real estate transaction?**

A. The time to complete the mortgage application

B. The time to conduct inspections and review documents

C. The time between listing and selling the property

D. The time to move out after the sale is complete

Answer: B

The due diligence period is the time during which the buyer has the opportunity to conduct inspections, review documents, and ensure they want to proceed with the purchase.

➡**29. What is "equity" in terms of real estate?**

A. The value of the property minus any loans against it

B. The initial down payment on a property

C. The interest rate on a mortgage

D. The profit from the sale of a property

Answer: A

Equity is the value of the property minus any loans or liens against it.

➡**30. What is a "balloon payment" in the context of a mortgage?**

A. A large payment made at the end of a loan term

B. A payment made to reduce interest rates

C. A payment made to extend the loan term

D. A payment made to initiate the loan

Answer: A

A balloon payment is a large payment that is due at the end of a balloon mortgage term, after smaller periodic payments have been made.

➡**31. What is the primary purpose of a "listing agreement"?**

A. To establish the buyer's intent

B. To formalize the relationship between seller and agent

C. To set the property price

D. To disclose property defects

Answer: B

A listing agreement formalizes the relationship between the seller and the real estate agent, outlining the terms and conditions of the property sale.

➡**32. What does "escrow" mean in a real estate transaction?**

A. A legal dispute

B. A neutral third party holding funds

C. A type of mortgage

D. A property inspection

Answer: B

Escrow refers to a neutral third party holding funds or documents until the transaction is completed.

➡**33. What is the main purpose of a "contingency" in a real estate contract?**

A. To speed up the sale

B. To provide an exit strategy for the buyer or seller

C. To set the commission rate

D. To establish a timeline for inspections

Answer: B

A contingency provides conditions under which a buyer or seller can back out of the contract without penalties.

➡️**34. What does "amortization" refer to in a mortgage context?**

A. The process of increasing property value

B. The process of paying off debt over time

C. The process of transferring property

D. The process of evaluating property

Answer: B

Amortization refers to the process of paying off debt over time through regular payments.

➡️**35. What is a "quitclaim deed"?**

A. A deed that transfers property with warranties

B. A deed that transfers property without warranties

C. A deed that nullifies a previous sale

D. A deed that establishes new property boundaries

Answer: B

A quitclaim deed transfers property without any warranties or guarantees, often used between family members or to clear title.

➡️**36. What does "underwriting" refer to in real estate?**

A. Evaluating a property's value

B. Evaluating a buyer's financial stability

C. Writing a property description

D. Writing a legal contract

Answer: B

Underwriting refers to the process of evaluating a buyer's financial stability to determine mortgage eligibility.

➡37. What is a "buyer's market"?

A. A market where prices are rising

B. A market where prices are falling

C. A market with more buyers than sellers

D. A market with more sellers than buyers

Answer: D

A buyer's market occurs when there are more sellers than buyers, often leading to lower prices.

➡38. What is "title insurance"?

A. Insurance against property damage

B. Insurance against title defects

C. Insurance against mortgage default

D. Insurance against property theft

Answer: B

Title insurance protects against financial loss due to defects in the title, such as liens or ownership disputes.

➡39. What is the "appraisal" in a real estate transaction?

A. A legal review

B. A property inspection

C. An estimate of property value

D. A mortgage evaluation

Answer: C

An appraisal is an estimate of a property's value, often required by lenders before approving a mortgage.

➡️ **40. What does "FSBO" stand for in real estate?**

A. For Sale By Owner

B. Fixed Sale Before Offer

C. Final Sale By Order

D. For Sale By Operator

Answer: A

FSBO stands for For Sale By Owner, indicating that the property is being sold without a real estate agent.

➡️ **41. What does "REO" stand for in real estate?**

A. Real Estate Operator

B. Real Estate Option

C. Real Estate Owned

D. Real Estate Offer

Answer: C

REO stands for Real Estate Owned, which refers to property owned by a lender after a foreclosure.

➡️ **42. What is the purpose of a "CMA" in real estate?**

A. To assess mortgage eligibility

B. To evaluate property value

C. To inspect the property

D. To verify the title

Answer: B

CMA stands for Comparative Market Analysis, which is used to evaluate the value of a property by comparing it to similar properties.

➡43. What is "redlining"?

A. A type of property survey

B. Discriminatory lending practices

C. A method of property valuation

D. A type of property insurance

Answer: B

Redlining refers to discriminatory lending practices where loans are denied based on the racial or ethnic composition of a neighborhood.

➡44. What is a "balloon mortgage"?

A. A mortgage with fluctuating interest rates

B. A mortgage with a large final payment

C. A mortgage with no down payment

D. A mortgage with a fixed interest rate

Answer: B

A balloon mortgage has smaller initial payments but requires a large lump-sum payment at the end of the term.

➡45. What is "zoning"?

   A. The process of dividing land

   B. The process of appraising land

   C. The process of selling land

   D. The process of transferring land

Answer: A

Zoning is the municipal or local government regulation that dictates how land in specific geographic zones can be used.

➡46. What does "PMI" stand for?

   A. Property Management Insurance

   B. Private Mortgage Insurance

   C. Property Market Index

   D. Public Mortgage Interest

Answer: B

PMI stands for Private Mortgage Insurance, which is often required when a down payment is less than 20%.

➡47. What is "staging" in real estate?

   A. Preparing legal documents

   B. Preparing the home for viewing

   C. Conducting an open house

   D. Conducting a property survey

Answer: B

Staging refers to preparing a home to make it appealing to potential buyers, often by using furniture and decor.

➡ 48. What is a "short sale"?

A. A quick sale process

B. A sale where the proceeds fall short of the debt owed

C. A sale with a reduced commission

D. A sale with a short contract period

Answer: B

A short sale occurs when the sale proceeds are less than the balance owed on the property's loan.

➡ 49. What is "equity" in real estate?

A. The value of the property minus debts

B. The initial down payment

C. The monthly mortgage payment

D. The final sale price

Answer: A

Equity is the value of the property minus any debts or liens against it.

➡ 50. What is the "right of first refusal" in a real estate context?

A. The right to refuse a sale after an inspection

B. The right to be the first to purchase a property before the owner sells it to someone else

C. The right to refuse to pay property taxes

D. The right to be the first to view a newly listed property

Answer: B

The "right of first refusal" gives an individual or entity the opportunity to purchase a property before the owner offers it for sale to the general public.

Contracts

Contracts are the cornerstone of any real estate transaction. They serve as the legal blueprint that outlines the rights, obligations, and expectations of each party involved. Whether you're a buyer, a seller, a landlord, or a tenant, understanding the intricacies of real estate contracts is crucial for anyone aspiring to be successful in the field. This chapter aims to delve deep into the world of real estate contracts, discussing their types, essential elements, special clauses, and other legal considerations that you should be aware of.

Types of Real Estate Contracts

- Purchase Agreements

This is the most common type of real estate contract. It outlines the terms and conditions under which a property will be sold. Elements like purchase price, earnest money deposit

amount, closing date, and contingencies are all specified in this agreement. Both parties must adhere to these terms, or risk legal consequences.

Contingencies in Purchase Agreements

Contingencies are conditions that must be met for the contract to proceed. Common contingencies include financing, home inspections, and appraisals. Failure to meet these conditions can result in the contract being voided, often without penalty to the buyer.

- Lease Agreements

Lease agreements are contracts between landlords and tenants that detail the terms of the rental property. These contracts specify rent amount, security deposit, length of the lease, and tenant responsibilities. They may also include clauses about pet ownership, maintenance, and grounds for eviction.

Types of Lease Agreements

- *Fixed-Term Lease:* A lease for a specific period, usually one year.
- *Month-to-Month Lease:* A lease that renews monthly and can be terminated by either party with proper notice.
- *Commercial Lease:* A lease for business purposes, often with different terms and legal requirements than residential leases.

- Option Agreements

Option agreements give potential buyers the right—but not the obligation—to purchase a property within a specified time frame at an agreed-upon price. These are often used in rent-to-own scenarios or land contracts.

- Land Contracts

Also known as "contracts for deed," these agreements allow the buyer to possess the property while making payments directly to the seller. Once the full price is paid, ownership is transferred.

Essential Elements of a Contract

Offer and Acceptance

For a contract to be valid, there must be a clear offer by one party and unequivocal acceptance by the other. This is often referred to as "mutual assent."

Consideration

This refers to something of value exchanged between parties. In real estate, this is often the property itself and the money paid for it.

Legality of Purpose

The contract must be for a legal purpose to be enforceable. For example, a contract to sell a property with a hidden meth lab would be void.

Competent Parties

All parties must be of sound mind, not under the influence of substances, and of legal age to enter into a contract.

Written and Signed

Most states require real estate contracts to be written and signed by both parties to be enforceable.

Special Clauses and Contingencies

Financing Clause

This clause provides a way out for buyers if they can't secure financing. It protects the buyer from losing their earnest money deposit if they fail to obtain a mortgage.

Inspection Clause

This allows the buyer to have the property inspected within a certain period. If significant issues are found, the buyer can renegotiate or withdraw without penalty.

Appraisal Clause

This ensures that the property must appraise at or above the sale price for the transaction to proceed. If it doesn't, the buyer can back out or renegotiate the price.

Force Majeure Clause

This clause allows parties to terminate the contract without penalty in the event of unforeseen disasters like earthquakes, floods, or pandemics.

Breach of Contract and Remedies

Specific Performance

The injured party can ask the court to enforce the terms of the contract, requiring the breaching party to fulfill their obligations.

Liquidated Damages

This is a predetermined amount that the breaching party must pay, often outlined in the contract itself.

Rescission

The contract is canceled, and any money or property exchanged is returned to the original owner.

State-Specific Regulations

Real estate laws can vary significantly from state to state. Always consult local laws and a legal advisor familiar with your jurisdiction.

Digital and Electronic Contracts

The rise of technology has led to the increasing use of digital contracts. E-signatures and online notaries are becoming more common, and these digital contracts are just as legally binding as paper ones.

Conclusion

Contracts are the backbone of all real estate transactions. They define the rules, set the stage for negotiations, and provide a legal framework for resolving disputes. Understanding the complexities of real estate contracts is not just a legal necessity but a critical component of successful real estate practice. Always consult with legal professionals for advice tailored to your specific situation.

Mock Exam Contracts

➡1. What is the most common type of real estate contract?

A. Lease Agreement

B. Purchase Agreement

C. Option Agreement

D. Land Contract

Answer: B

The most common type of real estate contract is the Purchase Agreement, which outlines the terms and conditions under which a property will be sold.

➡2. What is a contingency in a Purchase Agreement?

A. A penalty for late payment

B. A condition that must be met for the contract to proceed

C. A predetermined amount that the breaching party must pay

D. A clause that allows for digital signatures

Answer: B

Contingencies are conditions that must be met for the contract to proceed. They often include financing, home inspections, and appraisals.

➡3. What type of lease renews monthly?

A. Fixed-Term Lease

B. Month-to-Month Lease

C. Commercial Lease

D. None of the above

Answer: B

A Month-to-Month Lease renews monthly and can be terminated by either party with proper notice.

➡4. What does "Consideration" refer to in a contract?

A. Legal advice

B. Something of value exchanged between parties

C. A special clause

D. A type of contingency

Answer: B

Consideration refers to something of value exchanged between parties, such as the property itself and the money paid for it.

➡5. What makes a contract void?

A. If it is not written and signed

B. If it is for an illegal purpose

C. If it lacks an offer and acceptance

D. All of the above

Answer: D

A contract can be void for multiple reasons, including if it is for an illegal purpose, lacks an offer and acceptance, or is not written and signed.

➡6. What is a Financing Clause?

A. A clause that outlines the rent amount

B. A clause that provides a way out for buyers if they can't secure financing

C. A clause that allows for digital signatures

D. A clause that specifies the length of the lease

Answer: B

A Financing Clause provides a way out for buyers if they can't secure financing, protecting them from losing their earnest money deposit.

➡7. What is Specific Performance?

A. A type of contingency

B. A predetermined amount that the breaching party must pay

C. The court enforcing the terms of the contract

D. A type of lease agreement

Answer: C

Specific Performance is when the injured party can ask the court to enforce the terms of the contract, requiring the breaching party to fulfill their obligations.

➡8. What does a Force Majeure Clause allow?

A. Early termination of the lease

B. Parties to terminate the contract without penalty in the event of unforeseen disasters

C. The seller to keep the earnest money deposit

D. The buyer to renegotiate the price

Answer: B

A Force Majeure Clause allows parties to terminate the contract without penalty in the event of unforeseen disasters like earthquakes, floods, or pandemics.

➡9. What is the term for a lease for business purposes?

A. Fixed-Term Lease

B. Month-to-Month Lease

C. Commercial Lease

D. Option Agreement

Answer: C

A Commercial Lease is a lease for business purposes, often with different terms and legal requirements than residential leases.

➡ **10. What is an Option Agreement commonly used for?**

    A. Rent-to-own scenarios

    B. Short-term rentals

    C. Commercial properties

    D. Vacation rentals

Answer: A

Option Agreements are often used in rent-to-own scenarios or land contracts, giving potential buyers the right—but not the obligation—to purchase a property within a specified time frame.

➡ **11. What does a "contingency clause" in a contract allow?**

    A. The buyer to back out if financing falls through

    B. The seller to increase the price

    C. The buyer to take immediate possession

    D. The seller to back out if a better offer is received

Answer: A

A contingency clause allows for specific conditions that must be met for the contract to be binding. In this case, it allows the buyer to back out if they can't secure financing.

➡ **12. What is the primary purpose of a "listing agreement"?**

    A. To define the terms between the buyer and the mortgage lender

    B. To define the terms between the seller and the real estate agent

    C. To define the terms between the buyer and the seller

    D. To define the terms between the real estate agent and the mortgage lender

Answer: B

A listing agreement primarily outlines the terms and conditions under which a real estate agent will sell a property for a seller.

➡13. What does "specific performance" mean in a real estate contract?

    A. The buyer must secure financing within 30 days

    B. The seller must repair any defects before closing

    C. The buyer or seller must fulfill the contract terms or face legal consequences

    D. The real estate agent must meet sales targets

Answer: C

Specific performance means that the parties in the contract must perform their respective duties as specified in the contract, or they could face legal action.

➡14. What is the role of a "title company" in a real estate transaction?

    A. To market the property

    B. To secure financing for the buyer

    C. To ensure the title is clear and prepare for its transfer

    D. To inspect the property for defects

Answer: C

The title company ensures that the title to a piece of real estate is legitimate and prepares the necessary documents for the transfer of the property.

➡15. What is an "option contract" in real estate?

    A. A contract that allows the buyer to rent before purchasing

    B. A contract that allows the seller to find a better offer

    C. A contract that allows the buyer a specified time to decide on purchase

    D. A contract that binds both parties unconditionally

Answer: C

An option contract gives the buyer a certain period during which they can choose to purchase the property under pre-arranged terms, but are not obligated to do so.

➡16. What does "time is of the essence" mean in a contract?

    A. The contract has no expiration date

    B. Deadlines must be strictly adhered to

    C. The contract can be modified at any time

    D. Both parties have unlimited time to fulfill their obligations

Answer: B

"Time is of the essence" means that all deadlines are firm and must be strictly followed, otherwise, the party may be in breach of contract.

➡17. What is the purpose of an "earnest money deposit"?

    A. To pay the real estate agent's commission

    B. To show the buyer's serious intent to purchase

    C. To cover the cost of property inspection

    D. To pay for the property's closing costs

Answer: B

An earnest money deposit is made by the buyer to show their serious intent to complete the purchase, and it's usually held in an escrow account until closing.

➡18. What is "liquidated damages" in the context of a real estate contract?

    A. Money held in escrow

    B. Money earned from the sale

    C. Pre-determined compensation for a breach of contract

    D. Money returned to the buyer if the sale falls through

Answer: C

Liquidated damages are a predetermined amount of money that one party agrees to pay the other in the event of a breach of contract.

➡19. What is a "right of first refusal" clause?

    A. It allows the seller to accept a better offer

    B. It allows the buyer to match any offer the seller receives

    C. It allows the buyer to back out without penalty

    D. It allows the seller to back out if they receive a higher appraisal

Answer: B

A right of first refusal clause gives the buyer the opportunity to match any offer the seller receives before the property is sold to someone else.

➡20. What is a "bilateral contract"?

    A. A contract where only one party is obligated to perform

    B. A contract where both parties are obligated to perform

    C. A contract that is not legally binding

    D. A contract that can be broken without penalty

Answer: B

In a bilateral contract, both parties are obligated to perform certain duties, making it mutually binding.

➡21. What does "rescission" mean in a real estate contract?

    A. Extension of the contract period

    B. Legal termination of the contract by either party

    C. Transfer of property ownership

    D. Payment of all outstanding fees

Answer: B

Rescission refers to the legal termination of a contract, effectively restoring both parties to their original positions before the contract was made.

➡ **22. What is the role of a "notary public" in a real estate contract?**

    A. To negotiate the terms

    B. To verify the identities of the signing parties

    C. To provide legal advice

    D. To conduct the property inspection

Answer: B

A notary public verifies the identities of the parties signing the contract, ensuring that the signatures are legitimate.

➡ **23. What is "consideration" in a contract?**

    A. A period for the buyer to reconsider the purchase

    B. Something of value exchanged between parties

    C. A clause that allows for contract modifications

    D. A detailed description of the property

Answer: B

Consideration is something of value that is exchanged between the parties to make the contract binding, such as money, services, or a promise to perform a service.

➡ **24. What is a "unilateral contract"?**

    A. A contract where only one party is obligated to perform

    B. A contract where both parties are obligated to perform

    C. A contract that is not legally binding

    D. A contract that can be broken without penalty

Answer: A

In a unilateral contract, only one party is obligated to perform, while the other has the option but not the obligation to perform.

➡ 25. What does "novation" mean in a real estate contract?

    A. Adding a co-buyer to the contract

    B. Replacing one party in the contract with another

    C. Extending the contract's expiration date

    D. Changing the property's listing price

Answer: B

Novation involves replacing one party in a contract with another, effectively transferring the obligations to the new party.

➡ 26. What is a "due diligence period" in a real estate contract?

    A. The time for the buyer to inspect the property and secure financing

    B. The time for the seller to make necessary repairs

    C. The time for the real estate agent to market the property

    D. The time for the mortgage lender to approve the loan

Answer: A

The due diligence period allows the buyer time to inspect the property, secure financing, and complete any other tasks necessary before finalizing the purchase.

➡ 27. What is "specific performance" in a real estate contract?

    A. A clause that allows the buyer to back out

    B. A legal remedy requiring the contract to be executed as agreed

    C. A penalty for late payment

    D. A bonus for early completion of the contract

Answer: B

Specific performance is a legal remedy that requires the contract to be executed exactly as agreed upon, usually when monetary damages are insufficient.

➡ **28. What is a "contingency" in a real estate contract?**

  A. A binding agreement
  B. A condition that must be met for the contract to proceed
  C. An optional add-on to the contract
  D. A penalty for breaching the contract

Answer: B

A contingency is a condition that must be fulfilled for the contract to proceed, such as a successful home inspection or securing financing.

➡ **29. What is "due diligence" in the context of a real estate contract?**

  A. The buyer's responsibility to thoroughly investigate the property
  B. The seller's responsibility to disclose all known issues
  C. The agent's responsibility to close the deal quickly
  D. The lender's responsibility to provide the best interest rates

Answer: A

Due diligence refers to the buyer's responsibility to thoroughly investigate the property before finalizing the purchase.

➡ **30. What is a "counteroffer" in a real estate contract?**

  A. An offer made in response to another offer
  B. The first offer made by the buyer
  C. An offer made by the seller to multiple buyers
  D. The final offer accepted by both parties

Answer: A

A counteroffer is an offer made in response to another offer, usually changing some terms or conditions.

➡️ **31. What is "equitable title" in a real estate contract?**

    A. Full ownership of the property

    B. A claim or right to the property

    C. A temporary title until full payment is received

    D. A shared ownership in the property

Answer: B

Equitable title refers to a claim or right to the property, usually established once a contract is in place but before the legal title is transferred.

➡️ **32. What is a "voidable contract"?**

    A. A contract that is not legally binding

    B. A contract that can be voided by one party

    C. A contract that has been terminated

    D. A contract that is missing essential elements

Answer: B

A voidable contract is a valid contract that can be voided at the option of one of the parties.

➡️ **33. What is "escrow" in the context of a real estate contract?**

    A. A type of mortgage

    B. A neutral third party holding funds or documents

    C. A down payment

    D. A legal dispute over property ownership

Answer: B

Escrow refers to a neutral third party that holds funds or documents until certain conditions of the contract are met.

➡ **34. What is "implied contract"?**

    A. A contract formed through the actions of the parties

    B. A written contract

    C. A contract that is assumed but not stated

    D. A contract that is legally unenforceable

Answer: A

An implied contract is formed through the actions or conduct of the parties involved, rather than through written or spoken words.

➡ **35. What is "ratification" in a real estate contract?**

    A. The formal approval of a contract

    B. The termination of a contract

    C. The modification of a contract

    D. The initial formation of a contract

Answer: A

Ratification is the formal approval or acceptance of a contract, making it legally binding.

➡ **36. What is "executed contract"?**

    A. A contract that has been fully performed by both parties

    B. A contract that has been signed but not yet fulfilled

    C. A contract that has been terminated

    D. A contract that is still in negotiations

Answer: A

An executed contract is one that has been fully performed by both parties, fulfilling all terms and conditions.

➡️37. What is "liquidated damages" in a real estate contract?

   A. A refundable deposit

   B. A penalty for breaching the contract

   C. A type of insurance

   D. A bonus for early completion

Answer: B

Liquidated damages are a predetermined amount of money that one party will pay to the other in case of a breach of contract.

➡️38. What is "novation" in a real estate contract?

   A. Adding a new clause

   B. Replacing one party with another

   C. Extending the contract duration

   D. Changing the property in question

Answer: B

Novation is the act of replacing one party in a contract with another, effectively transferring the obligations to the new party.

➡️39. What is "time is of the essence" in a real estate contract?

   A. A clause that sets a strict timeline for performance

   B. A suggestion for quick action

   C. A type of contingency

   D. A legal doctrine for contract interpretation

Answer: A

"Time is of the essence" is a clause that sets a strict timeline for the performance of certain actions within the contract.

➡️ 40. What is "unilateral contract"?

A. A contract that obligates only one party

B. A contract that obligates both parties

C. A contract that is not legally binding

D. A contract that is missing essential elements

Answer: A

A unilateral contract is a contract where only one party is obligated to perform an action.

➡️ 41. What is "mutual assent" in a real estate contract?

A. Both parties agree to the terms

B. Both parties have read the contract

C. Both parties have legal representation

D. Both parties have paid a deposit

Answer: A

Mutual assent means that both parties agree to the terms of the contract, making it legally binding.

➡️ 42. What is "parol evidence" in contract law?

A. Written evidence

B. Oral evidence

C. Photographic evidence

D. Digital evidence

Answer: B

Parol evidence refers to oral statements or agreements that are not included in the written contract.

➦43. What is "rescission" in a real estate contract?

    A. The formal approval of a contract

    B. The termination of a contract

    C. The modification of a contract

    D. The initial formation of a contract

Answer: B

Rescission is the termination or nullification of a contract, usually by mutual agreement or due to some defect.

➦44. What is "adhesion contract"?

    A. A contract that is negotiated between parties

    B. A standard form contract

    C. A contract that is not legally binding

    D. A contract that is missing essential elements

Answer: B

An adhesion contract is a standard form contract where one party sets the terms and the other party has little or no ability to negotiate.

➦45. What is "quasi-contract"?

    A. A contract formed through the actions of the parties

    B. A not legally binding agreement

    C. An obligation imposed by law

    D. A contract that is legally unenforceable

Answer: C

A quasi-contract is not a true contract but an obligation imposed by law to prevent unjust enrichment.

→46. What is "breach of contract"?

A. The formal approval of a contract

B. The termination of a contract

C. The violation of any term or condition

D. The initial formation of a contract

Answer: C

Breach of contract is the violation of any term or condition in the contract, which may give the injured party the right to legal remedies.

→47. What is "voidable contract" in real estate?

A. A contract that is not legally binding

B. A contract that can be nullified by one party

C. A contract that lacks essential elements

D. A contract that is illegal

Answer: B

A voidable contract is a contract that is generally binding and enforceable, but it may be rejected or nullified by one of the parties under certain conditions.

→48. What is "specific performance" in a real estate contract?

A. A monetary compensation for breach

B. A legal remedy requiring the contract to be performed

C. A clause specifying the quality of work

D. A type of contingency

Answer: B

Specific performance is a legal remedy that requires the breaching party to perform the contract as promised, rather than simply paying damages.

⇒49. What is "ratification" in contract law?

A. The formal approval or acceptance of a contract
B. The termination of a contract
C. The modification of a contract
D. The initial formation of a contract

Answer: A

Ratification is the formal approval or acceptance of a contract or action, making it legally binding.

⇒50. What is "duress" in the context of contracts?

A. A freely given consent
B. Consent given under pressure or threat
C. A legal doctrine for contract interpretation
D. A type of contingency in contracts

Answer: B

Duress refers to situations where one party gives consent under pressure or threat, which can make the contract voidable.

Real Estate Calculations

Real estate calculations are not just numbers; they are the backbone of all real estate transactions. Whether you're an agent, a broker, an investor, or an appraiser, understanding the math behind each deal is crucial. This chapter will delve deep into the essential calculations that you'll encounter in your real estate career, explaining not just how to do them, but also why they matter.

Property Valuation

- Comparative Market Analysis (CMA)

A Comparative Market Analysis (CMA) is the cornerstone of property valuation. It involves comparing the property in question to similar properties ("comparables" or "comps") that have recently sold in the area.

Formula:

Property Value = Average Price of Comparable Properties x (1 + Adjustment Factor)}

Why It Matters:

Understanding how to accurately perform a CMA can mean the difference between overpricing a property, causing it to sit on the market, or underpricing it and losing money.

- Capitalization Rate

The capitalization rate, or cap rate, is another essential metric for property valuation, particularly for income-generating properties.

Formula:

$$\text{Cap Rate} = \frac{Net\ Operating\ Income}{Current\ Market\ Value}$$

Why It Matters:

The cap rate gives you a quick way to compare the profitability of different investment properties.

Financing Calculations

- Mortgage Payments

Mortgage calculations are essential for both buyers and real estate professionals to understand.

Formula:

$$M = P \times \frac{r(1+r)^n}{(1+r)^n - 1}$$

Where :

M is the monthly payment,

P is the principal loan amount,

r is the monthly interest rate, and

n is the number of payments.

Why It Matters:

Knowing how to calculate mortgage payments allows you to assess the affordability of a property and helps in planning long-term finances.

- Loan-to-Value Ratio (LTV)

The Loan-to-Value ratio is a risk assessment metric that lenders use.

Formula:

$$LTV = \frac{Loan\ Amount}{Appraised\ Value}\ \text{x } 100$$

Why It Matters:

A high LTV ratio might mean a riskier loan from a lender's perspective, potentially requiring the borrower to purchase mortgage insurance.

Investment Calculations

- Return on Investment (ROI)

ROI is a measure of the profitability of an investment.

Formula:

$$ROI = \frac{Net\ Profit}{Cost\ of\ Investment}\text{x } 100$$

Why It Matters:

ROI gives you a snapshot of the investment's performance, helping you compare it against other investment opportunities.

- Cash-on-Cash Return

This metric gives you the annual return on your investment based on the cash flow and the amount of money you've invested.

Formula:

$$\text{Cash-on-Cash Return} = \frac{Annual\ Cash\ Flow}{Total\ Cash\ Invested}\ \text{x } 100$$

Why It Matters:

Cash-on-cash return is crucial for understanding the cash income you're generating compared to the cash invested, providing a more accurate picture of an investment's performance.

Area and Volume Calculations

- Square Footage

Square footage is the measure of an area, and it's one of the most basic calculations in real estate.

Formula:

Area = Length x Width

Why It Matters:
Square footage affects everything from listing prices to renovation costs, so getting it right is crucial.

- Cubic Footage

Cubic footage is often used in commercial real estate to determine the volume of a space.

Formula:

Volume = Length x Width x Height

Why It Matters:
In commercial settings, cubic footage can be essential for understanding how a space can be used.

Prorations and Commissions

- Prorations

Prorations are used to divide property taxes, insurance premiums, or other costs between the buyer and seller.

Formula:

$$\text{Proration Amount} = \frac{\textit{Annual Cost}}{365} \times \textbf{Number of Days}$$

Why It Matters:

Prorations ensure that both parties are only paying for their share of the costs during the time they own the property.

- Commission Calculation

Commissions are the lifeblood of most real estate agents and brokers.

Formula:

Commission = Sale Price x Commission Rate

Why It Matters:

Understanding how commissions are calculated can help agents set realistic business goals and expectations.

Conclusion

Mastering these calculations is not just a requirement for passing various real estate exams; it's a necessity for a successful career in real estate. This chapter has covered the essential calculations any real estate professional needs to understand.

Mock Exam Real Estate Calculations

➡1. **What is the formula for calculating the Loan-to-Value ratio?**

   A. Loan Amount / Appraised Value

   B. Appraised Value / Loan Amount

   C. Loan Amount × Appraised Value

   D. Appraised Value × Loan Amount

Answer: A

The Loan-to-Value ratio is calculated as Loan Amount divided by Appraised Value.

➡2. **What does ROI stand for?**

   A. Return On Investment

   B. Rate Of Interest

   C. Real Estate Opportunity

   D. Rate Of Inflation

Answer: A

ROI stands for Return On Investment, which measures the profitability of an investment.

➡3. **What is the formula for calculating square footage?**

   A. Length × Width

   B. Length × Height

   C. Length + Width

   D. Length / Width

Answer: A

Square footage is calculated by multiplying the length by the width of the area.

➡️4. What is the formula for calculating mortgage payments?

    A. $P \times (r(1+r)^n) / ((1+r)^n-1)$

    B. $P \times r \times n$

    C. $P / r \times n$

    D. $P \times n / r$

Answer: A

The formula for calculating mortgage payments is $P \times (r(1+r)^n) / ((1+r)^n-1)$.

➡️5. What is the formula for calculating the capitalization rate?

    A. Net Operating Income / Current Market Value

    B. Current Market Value / Net Operating Income

    C. Net Operating Income $\times$ Current Market Value

    D. Current Market Value $\times$ Net Operating Income

Answer: A

The capitalization rate is calculated as Net Operating Income divided by Current Market Value.

➡️6. What does CMA stand for in real estate calculations?

    A. Comparative Market Analysis

    B. Capital Market Assessment

    C. Current Market Appraisal

    D. Comparative Monetary Assessment

Answer: A

CMA stands for Comparative Market Analysis, used for property valuation.

➡7. **What is the formula for calculating Cash-on-Cash Return?**

A. Annual Cash Flow / Total Cash Invested × 100

B. Total Cash Invested / Annual Cash Flow × 100

C. Annual Cash Flow × Total Cash Invested

D. Total Cash Invested × Annual Cash Flow

Answer: A

Cash-on-Cash Return is calculated as Annual Cash Flow divided by Total Cash Invested, multiplied by 100.

➡8. **What is the formula for calculating prorations?**

A. Annual Cost / 365 × Number of Days

B. Annual Cost × 365 / Number of Days

C. Number of Days / Annual Cost × 365

D. Number of Days × Annual Cost / 365

Answer: A

Prorations are calculated as Annual Cost divided by 365, multiplied by the Number of Days.

➡9. **What is the formula for calculating cubic footage?**

A. Length × Width × Height

B. Length × Width

C. Length × Height

D. Width × Height

Answer: A

Cubic footage is calculated by multiplying the length, width, and height of the space.

➡10. **What is the formula for calculating commissions?**

A. Sale Price × Commission Rate

B. Commission Rate × Sale Price

C. Sale Price / Commission Rate

D. Commission Rate / Sale Price

Answer: A

Commissions are calculated as Sale Price multiplied by Commission Rate.

➡**11. What is the formula for calculating Gross Rent Multiplier (GRM)?**

A. Property Price / Gross Annual Rents

B. Gross Annual Rents / Property Price

C. Property Price × Gross Annual Rents

D. Gross Annual Rents × Property Price

Answer: A

The Gross Rent Multiplier (GRM) is calculated by dividing the property price by the gross annual rents.

➡**12. What is the formula for calculating depreciation?**

A. (Cost of the Property - Salvage Value) / Useful Life

B. (Salvage Value - Cost of the Property) / Useful Life

C. Cost of the Property × Salvage Value

D. Salvage Value × Cost of the Property

Answer: A

Depreciation is calculated by subtracting the salvage value from the cost of the property and dividing by its useful life.

➡**13. What does PITI stand for in mortgage calculations?**

A. Principal, Interest, Taxes, Insurance

B. Payment, Interest, Taxes, Insurance

C. Principal, Income, Taxes, Insurance

D. Payment, Income, Taxes, Insurance

Answer: A

PITI stands for Principal, Interest, Taxes, and Insurance, which are the four components of a mortgage payment.

➡14. What is the formula for calculating equity?

A. Market Value - Mortgage Balance

B. Mortgage Balance - Market Value

C. Market Value × Mortgage Balance

D. Mortgage Balance × Market Value

Answer: A

Equity is calculated as the market value of the property minus the mortgage balance.

➡15. What is the formula for calculating net operating income (NOI)?

A. Gross Income - Operating Expenses

B. Operating Expenses - Gross Income

C. Gross Income × Operating Expenses

D. Operating Expenses × Gross Income

Answer: A

Net Operating Income (NOI) is calculated by subtracting operating expenses from gross income.

➡16. What is the formula for calculating the break-even point?

A. Fixed Costs / (Selling Price - Variable Costs)

B. (Selling Price - Variable Costs) / Fixed Costs

C. Fixed Costs × (Selling Price - Variable Costs)

D. (Selling Price - Variable Costs) × Fixed Costs

Answer: A

The break-even point is calculated by dividing fixed costs by the difference between the selling price and variable costs.

➡17. What is the formula for calculating the internal rate of return (IRR)?

A. NPV = 0

B. ROI = 100%

C. NPV × ROI

D. ROI × NPV

Answer: A

The internal rate of return (IRR) is the discount rate that makes the net present value (NPV) of all cash flows equal to zero.

➡18. What is the formula for calculating the price per square foot?

A. Total Price / Total Square Footage

B. Total Square Footage / Total Price

C. Total Price × Total Square Footage

D. Total Square Footage × Total Price

Answer: A.

The price per square foot is calculated by dividing the total price by the total square footage.

➡19. What is the formula for calculating the amortization schedule?

A. $P \times (r(1+r)^n) / ((1+r)^n - 1)$

B. $P \times r \times n$

C. $P / r \times n$

D. $P \times n / r$

Answer: A

The formula for calculating the amortization schedule is $P \times (r(1+r)^n) / ((1+r)^n-1)$.

➡20. What is the formula for calculating the future value of an investment?

A. $P \times (1 + r)^n$

B. $P \times (1 - r)^n$

C. $P / (1 + r)^n$

D. $P / (1 - r)^n$

Answer: A

The future value of an investment is calculated as $P \times (1 + r)^n$.

➡21. How do you calculate the Net Operating Income (NOI) for a property?

A. Gross Income - Operating Expenses

B. Gross Income + Operating Expenses

C. Operating Expenses - Gross Income

D. Gross Income × Operating Expenses

Answer: A

Net Operating Income is calculated by subtracting the operating expenses from the gross income.

➡22. What is the formula for calculating the loan-to-value ratio (LTV)?

A. Mortgage Amount / Appraised Value

B. Appraised Value / Mortgage Amount

C. Mortgage Amount × Appraised Value

D. Appraised Value × Mortgage Amount

Answer: A

The loan-to-value ratio (LTV) is calculated by dividing the mortgage amount by the appraised value of the property.

➡️**23. What is the formula for calculating the cash-on-cash return?**

A. Annual Pre-tax Cash Flow / Total Cash Invested

B. Total Cash Invested / Annual Pre-tax Cash Flow

C. Annual Pre-tax Cash Flow × Total Cash Invested

D. Total Cash Invested × Annual Pre-tax Cash Flow

Answer: A

The cash-on-cash return is calculated by dividing the annual pre-tax cash flow by the total cash invested.

➡️**24. What is the formula for calculating the debt service coverage ratio (DSCR)?**

A. Net Operating Income / Debt Service

B. Debt Service / Net Operating Income

C. Net Operating Income × Debt Service

D. Debt Service × Net Operating Income

Answer: A

The debt service coverage ratio (DSCR) is calculated by dividing the net operating income by the debt service.

➡️**25. What is the formula for calculating the equity build-up rate?**

A. (Principal Paid in Year 1 / Initial Investment) × 100

B. (Initial Investment / Principal Paid in Year 1) × 100

C. Principal Paid in Year 1 × Initial Investment

D. Initial Investment × Principal Paid in Year 1

Answer: A

The equity build-up rate is calculated by dividing the principal paid in the first year by the initial investment and then multiplying by 100.

➠26. **What is the formula for calculating the gross operating income (GOI)?**

A. Gross Potential Income - Vacancy and Credit Losses

B. Vacancy and Credit Losses - Gross Potential Income

C. Gross Potential Income × Vacancy and Credit Losses

D. Vacancy and Credit Losses × Gross Potential Income

Answer: A

The gross operating income (GOI) is calculated by subtracting vacancy and credit losses from the gross potential income.

➠27. **What is the formula for calculating the effective gross income (EGI)?**

A. Gross Operating Income + Other Income

B. Other Income - Gross Operating Income

C. Gross Operating Income × Other Income

D. Other Income × Gross Operating Income

Answer: A

The effective gross income (EGI) is calculated by adding other income to the gross operating income.

➠28. **What is the formula for calculating the absorption rate?**

A. Number of Units Sold / Number of Units Available

B. Number of Units Available / Number of Units Sold

C. Number of Units Sold × Number of Units Available

D. Number of Units Available × Number of Units Sold

Answer: A

The absorption rate is calculated by dividing the number of units sold by the number of units available.

➡29. What is the formula for calculating the price-to-rent ratio?

A. Home Price / Annual Rent

B. Annual Rent / Home Price

C. Home Price × Annual Rent

D. Annual Rent × Home Price

Answer: A

The price-to-rent ratio is calculated by dividing the home price by the annual rent.

➡30. What is the formula for calculating the yield?

A. Annual Income / Investment Cost

B. Investment Cost / Annual Income

C. Annual Income × Investment Cost

D. Investment Cost × Annual Income

Answer: A

The yield is calculated by dividing the annual income by the investment cost.

➡31. What is the formula for calculating the Gross Rent Multiplier (GRM)?

A. Sales Price / Monthly Rent

B. Monthly Rent / Sales Price

C. Sales Price × Monthly Rent

D. Monthly Rent × Sales Price

Answer: A

The Gross Rent Multiplier (GRM) is calculated by dividing the sales price by the monthly rent.

➡32. How do you calculate the Loan-to-Value ratio (LTV)?

A. Loan Amount / Appraised Value

B. Appraised Value / Loan Amount

C. Loan Amount × Appraised Value

D. Appraised Value × Loan Amount

Answer: A

The Loan-to-Value ratio (LTV) is calculated by dividing the loan amount by the appraised value of the property.

➡33. How do you calculate the Net Operating Income (NOI)?

A. Gross Operating Income - Operating Expenses

B. Operating Expenses - Gross Operating Income

C. Gross Operating Income × Operating Expenses

D. Operating Expenses × Gross Operating Income

Answer: A

The Net Operating Income (NOI) is calculated by subtracting the operating expenses from the gross operating income.

➡34. How do you calculate the Debt Service Coverage Ratio (DSCR)?

A. Net Operating Income / Debt Service

B. Debt Service / Net Operating Income

C. Net Operating Income × Debt Service

D. Debt Service × Net Operating Income

Answer: A

The Debt Service Coverage Ratio (DSCR) is calculated by dividing the Net Operating Income by the Debt Service.

➡35. What is the formula for calculating the Break-Even Ratio (BER)?

A. (Operating Expenses + Debt Service) / Gross Operating Income

B. Gross Operating Income / (Operating Expenses + Debt Service)

C. (Operating Expenses + Debt Service) × Gross Operating Income

D. Gross Operating Income × (Operating Expenses + Debt Service)

Answer: A

The Break-Even Ratio (BER) is calculated by dividing the sum of operating expenses and debt service by the gross operating income.

➡36. How do you calculate the Effective Gross Income (EGI)?

A. Gross Income - Vacancy Losses + Other Income

B. Gross Income + Vacancy Losses - Other Income

C. Gross Income × Vacancy Losses + Other Income

D. Gross Income + Vacancy Losses × Other Income

Answer: A

The Effective Gross Income (EGI) is calculated by subtracting vacancy losses from the gross income and adding any other income.

➡37. What is the formula for calculating the Operating Expense Ratio (OER)?

A. Operating Expenses / Effective Gross Income

B. Effective Gross Income / Operating Expenses

C. Operating Expenses × Effective Gross Income

D. Effective Gross Income × Operating Expenses

Answer: A

The Operating Expense Ratio (OER) is calculated by dividing the operating expenses by the effective gross income.

➡**38. How do you calculate the Cash-on-Cash Return?**

A. Cash Flow Before Taxes / Initial Investment

B. Initial Investment / Cash Flow Before Taxes

C. Cash Flow Before Taxes × Initial Investment

D. Initial Investment × Cash Flow Before Taxes

Answer: A

The Cash-on-Cash Return is calculated by dividing the cash flow before taxes by the initial investment.

➡**39. What is the formula for calculating the Amortization Factor?**

A. Monthly Payment / Loan Amount

B. Loan Amount / Monthly Payment

C. Monthly Payment × Loan Amount

D. Loan Amount × Monthly Payment

Answer: A

The Amortization Factor is calculated by dividing the monthly payment by the loan amount.

➡**40. How do you calculate the Equity Dividend Rate (EDR)?**

A. Cash Flow After Taxes / Equity Investment

B. Equity Investment / Cash Flow After Taxes

C. Cash Flow After Taxes × Equity Investment

D. Equity Investment × Cash Flow After Taxes

➡41. What is the formula for calculating the Debt Service Coverage Ratio (DSCR)?

A. Net Operating Income / Debt Service

B. Debt Service / Net Operating Income

C. Net Operating Income × Debt Service

D. Debt Service - Net Operating Income

Answer: A

The Debt Service Coverage Ratio is calculated by dividing the Net Operating Income by the Debt Service.

➡42. How do you calculate the Gross Rent Multiplier (GRM)?

A. Property Price / Monthly Rent

B. Monthly Rent / Property Price

C. Annual Rent / Property Price

D. Property Price / Annual Rent

Answer: A

The Gross Rent Multiplier is calculated by dividing the property price by the monthly rent.

➡43. What is the formula for calculating Loan-to-Value ratio?

A. Loan Amount / Property Value

B. Property Value / Loan Amount

C. Loan Amount × Property Value

D. Property Value - Loan Amount

Answer: A

The Loan-to-Value ratio is calculated by dividing the loan amount by the property value.

➡️**44. How do you calculate the break-even point in a real estate investment?**

    A. Fixed Costs / (Selling Price - Variable Costs)

    B. (Selling Price - Variable Costs) / Fixed Costs

    C. Fixed Costs × Selling Price

    D. Selling Price / Fixed Costs

Answer: A

The break-even point is calculated by dividing the fixed costs by the difference between the selling price and variable costs.

➡️**45. How do you calculate the Return on Investment (ROI) for a property?**

    A. (Net Profit / Investment Cost) × 100

    B. (Investment Cost / Net Profit) × 100

    C. Net Profit × Investment Cost

    D. Investment Cost - Net Profit

Answer: A

The Return on Investment is calculated by dividing the net profit by the investment cost and then multiplying by 100.

➡️**46. How do you calculate the equity in a property?**

    A. Property Value - Mortgage Balance

    B. Mortgage Balance - Property Value

    C. Property Value × Mortgage Balance

    D. Mortgage Balance / Property Value

Answer: A

Equity is calculated by subtracting the mortgage balance from the property value.

➡️47. What is the formula for calculating the amortization payment?

    A. Principal Amount / Number of Payments

    B. Interest Rate / Number of Payments

    C. (Principal Amount × Interest Rate) / Number of Payments

    D. (Principal Amount × Interest Rate) / (1 - (1 + Interest Rate)^-Number of Payments)

Answer: D

The amortization payment is calculated using the formula mentioned.

➡️48. What is the formula for calculating the Internal Rate of Return (IRR) for a real estate investment?

    A. The discount rate that makes the Net Present Value zero

    B. The rate that equals the Net Operating Income

    C. The rate that equals the Debt Service

    D. The rate that makes the Gross Income zero

Answer: A

The Internal Rate of Return is the discount rate that makes the Net Present Value of all cash flows from a particular investment equal to zero.

➡️49. What is the formula for calculating the rate of return on an investment property?

    A. (Net Profit / Cost of Investment) × 100

    B. (Cost of Investment / Net Profit) × 100

    C. Net Profit × Cost of Investment

D. Cost of Investment - Net Profit

Answer: A

The rate of return is calculated by dividing the net profit by the cost of the investment and then multiplying by 100.

➡**50. How do you calculate the net profit from a real estate investment?**

  A. Selling Price - (Buying Price + Costs)

  B. (Buying Price + Costs) - Selling Price

  C. Selling Price × Buying Price

  D. Buying Price / Selling Price

Answer: A

The Net Operating Income (NOI) is calculated by subtracting the operating expenses from the gross operating income.

Specialty Areas

The real estate industry is a multifaceted arena, offering a plethora of opportunities for professionals to specialize in various niches. While residential real estate is often the first thing that comes to mind, the industry is far more expansive. This chapter aims to delve deep into the various specialty areas within real estate, offering a comprehensive guide for those looking to specialize or diversify their real estate careers.

Residential Real Estate

Overview
Residential real estate is the most common form of real estate, involving the buying, selling, and renting of properties designed for individual or family living. These properties can range from single-family homes to multi-unit apartment buildings.

Types of Residential Properties:
- *Single-Family Homes:* Standalone houses with yards.
- *Condominiums:* Individual units in a larger complex.
- *Townhouses:* Multi-floor homes that share one or two walls with other similar homes.
- *Multi-Family Homes:* Buildings designed to house more than one family.

Market Trends
Understanding local market conditions, such as the average selling price and how long homes stay on the market, is crucial for success in residential real estate.

Commercial Real Estate

Overview
Commercial real estate focuses on business properties, including office buildings, retail spaces, and industrial properties. Transactions are often more complex and involve larger sums of money.

Types of Commercial Properties:

- *Office Spaces:* Buildings or parts of buildings used for conducting business.
- *Retail Stores:* Properties used for the sale of goods to consumers.
- *Warehouses:* Large buildings used for storing goods.

Leasing vs. Buying

Each has its pros and cons depending on the business needs. Leasing offers more flexibility, while buying is a long-term investment.

Industrial Real Estate

Overview

Industrial real estate involves properties used for manufacturing, production, and other industrial purposes. These properties often have specific zoning requirements and offer features like high ceilings, large doors, and loading docks.

Types of Industrial Properties:

- *Factories:* Where goods are manufactured.
- *Warehouses:* Where goods are stored or distributed.
- *Research Centers:* Where scientific research and development occur.

Zoning Laws

Industrial properties often have specific zoning requirements that must be met, including environmental regulations and restrictions on types of activities that can occur on the property.

Real Estate Investment

Overview

Investing in real estate can be a lucrative venture. This specialty area focuses on buying properties to generate a return on investment either through rental income, future resale, or both.

Types of Investments:

- *Rental Properties:* Buying properties to rent them out for income.
- *Flipping Houses:* Buying properties to renovate and sell for a profit.
- *Real Estate Investment Trusts (REITs):* Investing in a company that owns, operates, or finances real estate.

Risk and Return

Understanding the risk associated with different types of investments is crucial. Rental properties offer steady income but require ongoing management, while flipping houses can offer quick returns but come with higher risks.

Property Management

Overview

Property management involves the operation, control, and oversight of real estate. This includes everything from maintenance and rent collection to tenant relations and legal compliance.

Responsibilities:

- *Maintenance:* Ensuring the property is in good condition.
- *Rent Collection:* Managing income from tenants.
- *Tenant Relations:* Handling tenant issues and concerns.

Skills Required

Good communication, organizational skills, and a deep understanding of laws related to property management are essential for success in this area.

Land and Farm Real Estate

Overview

This specialty area focuses on undeveloped land, farms, and ranches. Agents must have a deep understanding of land use, zoning laws, and natural resources.

Types of Land and Farm Real Estate:

- *Agricultural Land:* Used for farming or ranching.

- *Undeveloped Land:* Land that has not been developed yet.

- *Ranches:* Large pieces of land geared toward livestock.

Considerations

Important considerations include soil quality, water rights, and land use restrictions.

Luxury Real Estate

Overview

Luxury real estate involves high-value homes and properties, often in exclusive locations. Agents must be knowledgeable about luxury market trends and the unique needs of high-net-worth individuals.

Types of Luxury Properties:

- *Mansions:* Large, opulent homes.

- *Penthouses:* Luxury apartments on the top floor of high-rise buildings.

- *Historic Homes:* Homes with historical significance and unique architectural features.

Market Trends

Luxury markets often behave differently from general real estate markets, with different factors affecting supply and demand.

Conclusion

The real estate industry is incredibly diverse, offering a range of specialty areas for those looking to carve out a niche. By understanding these specialty areas, you can make a more informed decision about which path to take in your real estate career. Each specialty comes with its own set of challenges, rewards, and required skill sets. Whether you're a seasoned professional or a newcomer to the industry, there's a specialty area in real estate that's perfect for you.

Mock Exam Specialty Areas

➡ **1. What is the primary focus of industrial real estate?**

   A. Retail sales

   B. Manufacturing and production

   C. Residential living

   D. Farming

   Answer: B

Industrial real estate is primarily used for manufacturing and production activities.

➡ **2. What type of real estate is most likely to include amenities like a swimming pool, gym, and community hall?**

   A. Commercial

   B. Residential

   C. Industrial

   D. Agricultural

   Answer: B

Residential real estate is most likely to include amenities like a swimming pool, gym, and community hall for the convenience and enjoyment of residents.

➡ **3. In retail real estate, what does "footfall" refer to?**

   A. The size of the property

   B. The number of people who enter the premises

   C. The cost per square foot

   D. The length of the lease

Answer: B

In retail real estate, "footfall" refers to the number of people who enter the premises, which is crucial for retail success.

➡4. What is the primary purpose of a real estate appraiser in commercial properties?

   A. To manage the property

   B. To determine the market value of the property

   C. To sell the property

   D. To lease out spaces

Answer: B

The primary purpose of a real estate appraiser in commercial properties is to determine the market value of the property.

➡5. What is the primary purpose of agricultural real estate?

   A. Manufacturing

   B. Farming and cultivation

   C. Retail sales

   D. Office work

Answer: B

Agricultural real estate is primarily used for farming and cultivation of land.

➡6. What type of property is primarily used for vacation purposes?

   A. Commercial

   B. Residential

   C. Recreational

   D. Industrial

Answer: C

Recreational properties are primarily used for vacation or leisure activities.

➡7. What is the main focus of a property manager in a residential setting?

   A. Increasing stock value

   B. Tenant satisfaction and maintenance

   C. Sales and marketing

   D. Manufacturing

Answer: B

In a residential setting, a property manager focuses on tenant satisfaction and maintenance of the property.

➡8. In commercial real estate, what is a triple net lease?

   A. A lease where the tenant pays rent only

   B. A lease where the tenant pays rent, utilities, and insurance

   C. A lease where the tenant pays rent, taxes, and maintenance

   D. A lease where the tenant pays rent, taxes, maintenance, and insurance

Answer: D

In a triple net lease, the tenant is responsible for rent, taxes, maintenance, and insurance.

➡9. What is the main advantage of investing in REITs (Real Estate Investment Trusts)?

   A. Direct control over properties

   B. Liquidity

   C. No need for property management

   D. All of the above

Answer: B

The main advantage of REITs is liquidity, as they can be bought and sold like stocks.

➡10. What type of specialty real estate focuses on the needs of the elderly?

   A. Commercial

   B. Agricultural

   C. Senior Housing

   D. Industrial

Answer: C

Senior Housing focuses on the specific needs of the elderly, providing facilities and services tailored to them.

➡11. What is the primary advantage of investing in a Real Estate Investment Trust (REIT)?

   A. Tax benefits

   B. Liquidity

   C. Control over property

   D. No risk

Answer: B

REITs offer the advantage of liquidity, allowing investors to easily buy and sell shares.

➡12. In a hotel property, what does RevPAR stand for?

   A. Revenue Per Available Room

   B. Real Estate Value Assessment

   C. Revenue Per Annual Report

   D. Room Expense Value Added

Answer: A

RevPAR stands for Revenue Per Available Room, a key performance metric in the hotel industry.

➡13. What type of real estate primarily focuses on income-producing properties?

A. Commercial

B. Residential

C. Industrial

D. Agricultural

Answer: A

Commercial real estate focuses primarily on income-producing properties like offices, retail spaces, and warehouses.

➡14. What is a triple net lease?

A. A lease where the tenant pays rent, utilities, and maintenance

B. A lease where the landlord pays all expenses

C. A lease that lasts for three years

D. A lease that can be terminated by either party after three months

Answer: A

In a triple net lease, the tenant is responsible for paying the rent as well as utilities and maintenance costs.

➡15. What is the primary focus of a real estate appraiser in the specialty area of valuation?

A. Market trends

B. Property condition

C. Comparable sales

D. Zoning laws

Answer: C

Appraisers primarily focus on comparable sales to determine a property's value.

➡ **16. In the context of retail real estate, what does "anchor tenant" mean?**

A. The first tenant in a property

B. A tenant occupying the largest space

C. A tenant with the shortest lease

D. A tenant who is late on rent

Answer: B

An anchor tenant is usually the largest tenant in a retail space and draws significant foot traffic.

➡ **17. What is the primary advantage of investing in industrial real estate?**

A. High liquidity

B. Long-term leases

C. Tax benefits

D. Low maintenance

Answer: B

Industrial real estate often comes with long-term leases, providing stable income.

➡ **18. What does "cap rate" stand for in real estate investment?**

A. Capital appreciation rate

B. Capitalization rate

C. Capital asset rate

D. Capital allocation rate

Answer: B

Cap rate stands for capitalization rate, a metric used to evaluate the potential return on an investment.

➡ **19. In property management, what does NOI stand for?**

A. Net Operating Income
B. No Outstanding Issues
C. Net Operational Interest
D. None of the Above

Answer: A

NOI stands for Net Operating Income, a key metric in property management to evaluate profitability.

➡ **20. What is the primary role of a real estate syndicator?**

A. Property management
B. Pooling investment funds
C. Legal advice
D. Construction

Answer: B

A real estate syndicator primarily pools funds from multiple investors for larger investments.

➡ **21. In a 1031 exchange, what is the maximum period to identify a replacement property?**

A. 30 days
B. 45 days
C. 60 days
D. 90 days

Answer: B

In a 1031 exchange, you have 45 days to identify a replacement property.

➡ **22. What does a real estate wholesaler do?**

A. Repairs and flips properties

B. Holds properties for rental income

C. Contracts to buy properties and assigns them to investors

D. Manages multiple properties

Answer: C

A real estate wholesaler contracts to buy properties and then assigns those contracts to investors.

➡ **23. What is the primary focus of a real estate developer?**

A. Buying and holding properties

B. Renovating existing properties

C. Creating new properties

D. Managing commercial properties

Answer: C

A real estate developer primarily focuses on creating new properties.

➡ **24. What is the main advantage of a sale-leaseback transaction for a business?**

A. Tax benefits

B. Liquidity

C. Control over property

D. Lower rent

Answer: B

A sale-leaseback can provide a business with liquidity by freeing up capital tied in real estate.

➡ 25. What is the primary disadvantage of investing in raw land?

A. High maintenance

B. Lack of liquidity

C. High property taxes

D. Zoning restrictions

Answer: B

Investing in raw land often comes with a lack of liquidity, making it harder to sell quickly.

➡ 26. What is the primary role of a real estate auctioneer?

A. Property management

B. Selling properties through a bidding process

C. Legal advice

D. Construction

Answer: B

A real estate auctioneer's primary role is to sell properties through a bidding process.

➡ 27. What is the main disadvantage of investing in vacation rentals?

A. Seasonal income

B. High maintenance

C. Zoning restrictions

D. High property taxes

Answer: A

The main disadvantage is seasonal income, which can be inconsistent

➡28. What is the primary advantage of investing in multi-family real estate?

A. Diversified income

B. Tax benefits

C. High liquidity

D. Low maintenance

Answer: A

Multi-family real estate provides diversified income from multiple tenants.

➡29. What is the primary focus of a real estate attorney?

A. Contract law

B. Property management

C. Construction

D. Investment pooling

Answer: A

A real estate attorney primarily focuses on contract law related to property transactions.

➡30. What does "NNN" stand for in a lease agreement?

A. No New Negotiations

B. Net Net Net

C. No Net Necessities

D. None of the Above

Answer: B

NNN stands for Net Net Net, which means the tenant is responsible for net real estate taxes, net building insurance, and net common area maintenance.

➡31. What is the primary disadvantage of investing in commercial real estate?

A. High maintenance

B. Complexity and risk

C. Zoning restrictions

D. Seasonal income

Answer: B

The primary disadvantage is the complexity and risk involved compared to residential real estate.

➡**32. What is the main advantage of a triple net lease for an investor?**

A. Lower rent

B. Tax benefits

C. Stable income

D. High liquidity

Answer: C

A triple net lease provides stable income as the tenant covers most of the costs.

➡**33. What is the primary role of a real estate consultant?**

A. Providing expert advice

B. Property management

C. Legal advice

D. Construction

Answer: A

A real estate consultant's primary role is to provide expert advice to clients.

➡**34. What is the primary focus of a real estate broker in commercial transactions?**

A. Contract negotiations

B. Property valuation

C. Marketing properties

D. Legal compliance

Answer: C

In commercial transactions, a real estate broker primarily focuses on marketing properties.

➡ **35. What is the main disadvantage of investing in REITs?**

A. Lack of control

B. Seasonal income

C. High maintenance

D. Zoning restrictions

Answer: A

The main disadvantage is the lack of control over the properties in the portfolio.

➡ **36. What is the primary advantage of investing in a Real Estate Investment Group (REIG)?**

A. Diversification

B. Tax benefits

C. High liquidity

D. Low entry cost

Answer: A

The primary advantage of a REIG is diversification, as it allows you to invest in multiple properties.

➡37. What is the main role of a property appraiser in a real estate transaction?

A. Legal advice

B. Property valuation

C. Marketing

D. Contract negotiation

Answer: B

A property appraiser's main role is to provide an accurate valuation of the property.

➡38. What is the primary disadvantage of investing in industrial real estate?

A. Complexity and risk

B. High maintenance costs

C. Zoning restrictions

D. Seasonal income

Answer: B

The primary disadvantage is the high maintenance costs associated with industrial properties.

➡39. What is the primary focus of a real estate wholesaler?

A. Contract assignment

B. Property management

C. Legal advice

D. Construction

Answer: A

A real estate wholesaler primarily focuses on contract assignment to end buyers.

➡40. What is the main advantage of a gross lease for a tenant?

A. Lower rent

B. Predictable costs

C. Tax benefits

D. High liquidity

Answer: B

A gross lease provides predictable costs as the landlord covers most of the property expenses.

➡️ **41. What is the primary advantage of a triple net lease for a landlord?**

A. Lower maintenance costs

B. Predictable income

C. Tax benefits

D. High liquidity

Answer: B

A triple net lease provides predictable income for the landlord, as the tenant is responsible for most property expenses.

➡️ **42. What is the main disadvantage of investing in retail real estate?**

A. High vacancy rates

B. Complexity and risk

C. Zoning restrictions

D. Seasonal income

Answer: A

The main disadvantage is the potential for high vacancy rates, especially in challenging economic times.

➡️ **43. What is the main disadvantage of investing in a Real Estate Investment Trust (REIT)?**

A. Lack of control

B. High maintenance costs

C. Zoning restrictions

D. Seasonal income

Answer: A

The main disadvantage of a REIT is the lack of control over the properties in the investment portfolio.

➡️**44. What is the main advantage of a net lease for a landlord?**

A. Lower maintenance costs

B. Tax benefits

C. Stable income

D. High liquidity

Answer: A

A net lease typically results in lower maintenance costs for the landlord.

➡️**45. What is the primary disadvantage of investing in office real estate?**

A. High maintenance costs

B. Complexity and risk

C. Long-term leases

D. Seasonal income

Answer: C

The primary disadvantage is the commitment to long-term leases, which may not always be favorable.

➡️**46. In a commercial lease, what does the term "CAM" stand for?**

A. Centralized Asset Management

B. Common Area Maintenance

C. Commercial Asset Markup

D. Capital Allocation Model

Answer: B

CAM stands for Common Area Maintenance, which are the costs that tenants might be responsible for in a commercial lease.

➡️**47. What is the primary focus of a property manager in a residential setting?**

A. Increasing property value

B. Tenant satisfaction

C. Tax planning

D. Zoning compliance

Answer: B

In a residential setting, the primary focus of a property manager is usually tenant satisfaction to ensure long-term occupancy and minimize turnover.

➡️**48. What is the main advantage of investing in vacation rentals?**

A. Tax benefits

B. High rental yields

C. Long-term tenants

D. Low maintenance

Answer: B

The main advantage of investing in vacation rentals is the potential for high rental yields, especially during peak seasons.

➡️**49. What is the primary role of a buyer's agent in a real estate transaction?**

A. To represent the seller

B. To negotiate the best price for the buyer

C. To inspect the property

D. To provide financing options

Answer: B

The primary role of a buyer's agent is to represent the buyer's interests and negotiate the best possible price for them.

⟶50. What is a 1031 exchange?

A. A tax-deferred property exchange

B. A type of mortgage

C. A zoning regulation

D. A type of REIT

Answer: A

A 1031 exchange is a tax-deferred property exchange that allows an investor to sell a property and reinvest the proceeds in a new property while deferring capital gains tax.

Ethics and Legal Considerations

Ethics and legal considerations are the backbone of any profession, and real estate is no exception. This chapter aims to provide a comprehensive understanding of the ethical and legal responsibilities that real estate professionals must uphold. From fiduciary duties to fair housing laws, we will delve into the intricacies that govern ethical conduct and legal obligations in the real estate industry.

Ethical Conduct in Real Estate

Fiduciary Duties

Real estate agents owe fiduciary duties to their clients, which include loyalty, confidentiality, obedience, full disclosure, and accounting. These duties are not just ethical guidelines but are often legally mandated.

Code of Ethics

Many real estate professionals are members of organizations like the National Association of Realtors (NAR), which has its own Code of Ethics. This code serves as a standard for ethical conduct, covering responsibilities towards clients, the public, and other realtors.

Honesty and Integrity

Honesty and integrity are not just moral virtues but are essential for building trust with clients. Misrepresentation or omission of property details can lead to legal repercussions.

Legal Considerations

Licensing Laws

Every state has its own set of licensing laws that real estate professionals must adhere to. These laws often require ongoing education and can result in penalties or loss of license for violations.

Fair Housing Laws

The Fair Housing Act prohibits discrimination based on race, color, religion, sex, or national origin. Some states have additional protections, such as sexual orientation and marital status.

Disclosure Requirements

Sellers and agents are required to disclose any known defects or issues with the property. Failure to do so can result in lawsuits and financial penalties.

Ethical and Legal Dilemmas

Dual Agency

Dual agency occurs when an agent represents both the buyer and the seller. While not illegal in all states, it presents an ethical dilemma as the agent has fiduciary duties to both parties.

Kickbacks and Referrals

Accepting kickbacks from service providers like home inspectors or mortgage brokers is both unethical and illegal. The Real Estate Settlement Procedures Act (RESPA) prohibits such practices.

Handling of Funds

Agents are often entrusted with earnest money deposits, which must be handled with extreme care. Misappropriation of these funds is both illegal and unethical.

Case Studies

Case Study 1: Fair Housing Violation

In 2019, a real estate agency in New York was sued for steering minority clients towards specific neighborhoods, a clear violation of the Fair Housing Act.

Case Study 2: Failure to Disclose

An agent in California failed to disclose that a property was located in a flood zone. The new homeowners sued the agent after their home was severely damaged in a flood.

Conclusion

Ethics and legal considerations in real estate are not just about following the law but also about fostering trust and integrity in all business dealings. Failure to adhere to these principles can result in not just legal consequences but also damage to reputation and loss of client trust.

Mock Exam Ethics and Legal Considerations

➡1. What is the primary purpose of the Fair Housing Act?

A. To regulate real estate agents

B. To prevent discrimination in housing

C. To set interest rates for mortgages

D. To establish zoning laws

Answer: B

The Fair Housing Act aims to prevent discrimination based on race, color, religion, sex, or national origin in housing.

➡2. Which of the following is NOT a fiduciary duty owed by a real estate agent to their client?

A. Loyalty

B. Confidentiality

C. Obedience

D. Profitability

Answer: D

Profitability is not a fiduciary duty. The fiduciary duties are loyalty, confidentiality, obedience, full disclosure, and accounting.

➡3. What does RESPA stand for?

A. Real Estate Settlement Procedures Act

B. Real Estate Sales Professional Act

C. Residential Estate Settlement Procedures Act

D. Real Estate Security Procedures Act

Answer: A

RESPA stands for Real Estate Settlement Procedures Act, which prohibits kickbacks and referrals among other things.

⇒4. What is dual agency?

A. When an agent represents both the buyer and the seller

B. When two agents work for the same client

C. When an agent works for two different real estate firms

D. When an agent sells both commercial and residential properties

Answer: A

Dual agency occurs when an agent represents both the buyer and the seller, which can present an ethical dilemma.

⇒5. Which organization has its own Code of Ethics for real estate professionals?

A. FBI

B. NAR

C. IRS

D. HUD

Answer: B

The National Association of Realtors (NAR) has its own Code of Ethics that serves as a standard for ethical conduct.

⇒6. What is the penalty for violating licensing laws?

A. A small fine

B. Loss of license

C. Mandatory re-education

D. Both B and C

Answer: D

Violating licensing laws can result in penalties, loss of license, and mandatory re-education.

➡️**7. What must sellers and agents disclose to potential buyers?**

A. Any known defects or issues with the property

B. The seller's reason for selling

C. The agent's commission rate

D. All of the above

Answer: A

Sellers and agents are legally required to disclose any known defects or issues with the property.

➡️**8. What is the primary ethical dilemma with dual agency?**

A. Time management

B. Fiduciary duties to both parties

C. Commission splitting

D. Legal liability

Answer: B

The primary ethical dilemma with dual agency is that the agent has fiduciary duties to both the buyer and the seller.

➡️**9. What does the Code of Ethics by NAR cover?**

A. Responsibilities towards clients

B. Responsibilities towards the public

C. Responsibilities towards other realtors

D. All of the above

Answer: D

The Code of Ethics by NAR covers responsibilities towards clients, the public, and other realtors.

➡️**10. What is the primary focus of the Real Estate Settlement Procedures Act (RESPA)?**

    A. Preventing discrimination

    B. Regulating real estate agents

    C. Prohibiting kickbacks and referrals

    D. Setting interest rates for mortgages

Answer: C

The primary focus of RESPA is to prohibit kickbacks and referrals among service providers in the real estate industry.

➡️**11. What is the primary role of the Equal Credit Opportunity Act (ECOA)?**

    A. To ensure fair lending practices

    B. To regulate real estate agents

    C. To establish zoning laws

    D. To set interest rates for mortgages

Answer: A

The Equal Credit Opportunity Act (ECOA) aims to ensure that all consumers have an equal chance to obtain credit.

➡️**12. What is puffing in real estate?**

    A. Exaggerating property features

    B. Concealing property defects

    C. Making false promises

D. All of the above

Answer: A

Puffing refers to the exaggeration of property features and is generally considered legal but ethically questionable.

➡**13. What is the primary focus of the Truth in Lending Act?**

A. To ensure transparency in lending practices

B. To regulate real estate agents

C. To establish zoning laws

D. To set interest rates for mortgages

Answer: A

The Truth in Lending Act aims to ensure transparency in lending practices by requiring full disclosure of loan terms and costs.

➡**14. What is the primary role of the Federal Trade Commission (FTC) in real estate?**

A. To ensure fair business practices

B. To regulate real estate agents

C. To establish zoning laws

D. To set interest rates for mortgages

Answer: A

The Federal Trade Commission (FTC) aims to ensure fair business practices, including in the real estate industry.

➡**15. What is the primary focus of the Sherman Antitrust Act in real estate?**

A. To prevent price-fixing

B. To regulate real estate agents

C. To establish zoning laws

D. To set interest rates for mortgages

Answer: A

The Sherman Antitrust Act aims to prevent price-fixing and promote fair competition.

➡️16. What is the primary role of the Real Estate Settlement Procedures Act (RESPA)?

A. To ensure transparency in closing costs

B. To regulate real estate agents

C. To establish zoning laws

D. To set interest rates for mortgages

Answer: A

The Real Estate Settlement Procedures Act (RESPA) aims to ensure transparency in closing costs for residential properties.

➡️17. What is the primary focus of the Americans with Disabilities Act (ADA) in real estate?

A. To ensure properties are accessible to people with disabilities

B. To regulate real estate agents

C. To establish zoning laws

D. To set interest rates for mortgages

Answer: A

The Americans with Disabilities Act (ADA) aims to ensure that public and commercial properties are accessible to people with disabilities.

➡️18. What is blockbusting?

A. Encouraging people to sell their homes by instilling fear of a changing neighborhood

B. Exaggerating property features

C. Concealing property defects

D. Making false promises

Answer: A

Blockbusting is the practice of encouraging people to sell their homes by instilling fear that the racial or social makeup of the neighborhood is changing.

➡19. What is redlining?

A. Discriminating against a buyer or seller based on race or ethnicity

B. Refusing to lend in certain areas based on demographics

C. Exaggerating property features

D. Making false promises

Answer: B

Redlining is the practice of refusing to lend in certain areas based on demographics, often targeting racial or ethnic communities.

➡20. What is steering?

A. Directing clients towards or away from certain neighborhoods based on race or ethnicity

B. Encouraging people to sell their homes by instilling fear of a changing neighborhood

C. Exaggerating property features

D. Making false promises

Answer: A

Steering is the practice of directing clients towards or away from certain neighborhoods based on race or ethnicity.

➡21. What is the primary purpose of the Truth in Lending Act (TILA)?

A. To protect consumers in loan transactions

B. To regulate real estate agents

C. To establish zoning laws

D. To set interest rates for mortgages

Answer: A

The Truth in Lending Act (TILA) aims to protect consumers by requiring clear disclosure of key terms in the lending arrangement and all costs.

➡**22. What is the role of the Federal Trade Commission (FTC) in real estate?**

A. To oversee real estate transactions

B. To enforce anti-trust laws

C. To establish zoning laws

D. To regulate mortgage lending

Answer: B

The Federal Trade Commission (FTC) enforces anti-trust laws, ensuring that business competitions are fair and free from collusion.

➡**23. What is the primary focus of the Fair Housing Act?**

A. To prevent discrimination in housing based on protected classes

B. To regulate real estate agents

C. To establish zoning laws

D. To set interest rates for mortgages

Answer: A

The Fair Housing Act aims to prevent discrimination in housing based on race, color, religion, sex, or national origin.

➡**24. What is a fiduciary duty?**

A. A legal obligation to act in the best interest of another

B. A requirement to disclose all property defects

C. A mandate to complete all transactions within a set timeframe

D. An obligation to pay taxes on a property

Answer: A

A fiduciary duty is a legal obligation to act in the best interest of another, often pertaining to a real estate agent's relationship with their client.

➡**25. What is puffing in real estate?**

A. Illegal exaggeration of property features

B. Legal exaggeration of property features

C. Concealing property defects

D. Making false promises

Answer: B

Puffing refers to the legal exaggeration of property features, often used as a sales tactic.

➡**25. What is the primary purpose of the Real Estate Settlement Procedures Act (RESPA)?**

A. To ensure consumers are provided with timely and accurate information during the real estate transaction process

B. To regulate mortgage lending

C. To establish zoning laws

D. To set interest rates for mortgages

Answer: A

The Real Estate Settlement Procedures Act (RESPA) aims to provide consumers with detailed information about estimated costs and to eliminate kickbacks or referral fees that could unnecessarily increase the costs of certain settlement services.

➠26. What is the primary role of the National Association of Realtors (NAR) in relation to ethics?

A. Enforce state laws

B. Create federal regulations

C. Establish and enforce a Code of Ethics

D. Provide legal representation for agents

Answer: C

The National Association of Realtors (NAR) is responsible for establishing and enforcing a Code of Ethics for its members.

➠27. What is the statute of frauds?

A. A law that requires certain contracts to be in writing

B. A law that deals with fraudulent activities in real estate

C. A law that sets the statute of limitations for fraud cases

D. A law that defines what constitutes fraud

Answer: A

The statute of frauds is a law that requires certain contracts, including real estate contracts, to be in writing to be enforceable.

➠28. What is the primary purpose of a fiduciary duty?

A. To protect the client's financial interests

B. To ensure the agent gets the highest commission

C. To protect the agent's financial interests

D. To ensure a quick sale

Answer: A

The primary purpose of a fiduciary duty is to protect the client's financial interests above all else.

→29. What does the term "puffing" refer to in real estate?

A. Exaggerated or superlative comments about property features

B. Inflating the price of a property

C. Falsifying property documents

D. Making false claims about property boundaries

Answer: A

"Puffing" refers to exaggerated or superlative comments about property features, which are not considered legally binding statements.

→30. What does "redlining" refer to?

A. Marking up a contract with changes

B. Discriminatory practice of denying loans in certain neighborhoods

C. Drawing property boundaries on a map

D. Marking areas on a map for zoning purposes

Answer: B

Redlining is the discriminatory practice of denying loans or insurance coverage in certain neighborhoods based on racial or ethnic composition.

→31. What is the purpose of a "disclosure statement" in a real estate transaction?

A. To disclose the agent's commission rate

B. To disclose any known defects or issues with the property

C. To disclose the buyer's financial information

D. To disclose zoning laws

Answer: B

The purpose of a disclosure statement is to disclose any known defects or issues with the property to the buyer.

➡32. What does RESPA not regulate?

A. Settlement procedures

B. Closing costs

C. Real estate agent commissions

D. Mortgage brokers

Answer: C

RESPA does not regulate real estate agent commissions.

➡33. What is "blockbusting"?

A. Encouraging people to sell their homes by instilling fear of a changing neighborhood demographic

B. Buying large blocks of property for development

C. Blocking certain buyers from viewing a property

D. Dividing a large property into smaller blocks for sale

Answer: A

Blockbusting is the practice of encouraging people to sell their homes by instilling fear of a changing neighborhood demographic, often for financial gain.

➡34. What does the Fair Housing Act prohibit?

A. Discrimination based on race, color, religion, sex, or national origin

B. Discrimination based on financial status

C. Discrimination based on occupation

D. Discrimination based on marital status

Answer: A

The Fair Housing Act prohibits discrimination in the sale, rental, and financing of dwellings based on race, color, religion, sex, or national origin.

➡️**35. What is the primary purpose of a "title search"?**

A. To search for the property's market value

B. To ensure the seller has the legal right to sell the property

C. To search for any liens on the property

D. To ensure the property meets zoning laws

Answer: B

The primary purpose of a title search is to ensure that the seller has the legal right to sell the property and that there are no undisclosed liens or other encumbrances.

➡️**36. What is the primary role of the Real Estate Commission in most states?**

A. To set property taxes

B. To regulate and license real estate agents

C. To mediate disputes between buyers and sellers

D. To set interest rates for mortgages

Answer: B

The primary role of the Real Estate Commission in most states is to regulate and license real estate agents.

➡️**37. What does the term "dual agency" refer to?**

A. Two agents representing the same client

B. One agent representing both the buyer and the seller

C. Two agents from the same brokerage representing opposing parties

D. Two buyers competing for the same property

Answer: B

Dual agency refers to a situation where one agent represents both the buyer and the seller in a real estate transaction.

→38. What is the purpose of an "earnest money deposit"?

A. To cover the agent's commission

B. To show the buyer's serious intent to purchase

C. To pay for the property inspection

D. To cover closing costs

Answer: B

The purpose of an earnest money deposit is to show the buyer's serious intent to purchase the property.

→39. What does "steering" refer to in a real estate context?

A. Guiding a buyer towards or away from certain neighborhoods based on discriminatory factors

B. Directing a seller to accept a specific offer

C. Advising a buyer on mortgage options

D. Directing traffic during an open house

Answer: A

Steering refers to the practice of guiding a buyer towards or away from certain neighborhoods based on discriminatory factors such as race, religion, or ethnicity.

→40. What is the "right of first refusal" in a lease agreement?

A. The right to refuse any subletting of the property

B. The right to be the first to purchase the property if the owner decides to sell

C. The right to refuse any changes to the lease terms

D. The right to be the first to renew the lease

Answer: B

The right of first refusal gives the lessee the opportunity to be the first to purchase the property if the owner decides to sell.

➟41. What is the "doctrine of caveat emptor"?

A. Buyer beware

B. Seller beware

C. Equal opportunity for all

D. Due diligence required

Answer: A

The doctrine of "caveat emptor" means "buyer beware," indicating that the buyer is responsible for checking the quality and suitability of goods before a purchase is made.

➟42. What is "chattel" in real estate?

A. Immovable property like land and buildings

B. Movable personal property

C. A type of mortgage

D. A legal contract between buyer and seller

Answer: B

In real estate, "chattel" refers to movable personal property that may be included in a sale, such as furniture or appliances.

➟43. What is a "contingency" in a real estate contract?

A. A binding clause

B. A non-negotiable term

C. A condition that must be met for the contract to be binding

D. A penalty for breach of contract

Answer: C

A contingency is a condition that must be met for the real estate contract to become binding, such as a satisfactory home inspection.

➡️44. What does "quiet enjoyment" refer to in a lease agreement?

A. The right to peace and quiet

B. The right to enjoy the property without disturbance from the landlord

C. The right to host parties and events

D. The right to sublet the property

Answer: B

Quiet enjoyment refers to the tenant's right to enjoy the property without disturbance from the landlord or other tenants.

➡️45. What is "adverse possession"?

A. Illegal occupation of a property

B. Gaining legal ownership of a property through continuous occupation

C. A negative easement affecting property value

D. A form of property foreclosure

Answer: B

Adverse possession is a legal principle that allows a person to gain ownership of a property through continuous, open, and notorious occupation.

➡️46. What is the "Red Flag Rule" in real estate?

A. A rule that requires agents to disclose known defects in a property

B. A rule that requires agents to identify and prevent identity theft

C. A rule that prohibits agents from discussing financing options

D. A rule that requires agents to use a specific type of contract

Answer: B

The "Red Flag Rule" requires real estate agents to have a written identity theft prevention program designed to detect the warning signs—or "red flags"—of identity theft in their day-to-day operations.

➡️**47. What does "procuring cause" refer to in a real estate transaction?**

A. The reason for a property's appreciation

B. The actions that result in the sale of a property

C. The cause of a contract breach

D. The source of financing for a property

Answer: B

Procuring cause refers to the series of events set in motion by the agent that result in the sale of a property.

➡️**48. What is the "Sherman Antitrust Act" concerned with?**

A. Environmental regulations

B. Monopolistic practices

C. Property zoning

D. Fair housing

Answer: B

The Sherman Antitrust Act is federal legislation aimed at preventing monopolistic practices and promoting competition among businesses, including real estate agencies.

➡️**49. What does "RESPA" stand for?**

A. Real Estate Settlement Procedures Act

B. Real Estate Sales Professional Agreement

C. Residential Equity Sales Property Act

D. Real Estate Security Provision Act

Answer: A

RESPA stands for Real Estate Settlement Procedures Act, which requires lenders to provide homebuyers with information about known or estimated settlement costs.

➡**50. What is the primary purpose of a "fiduciary duty" in real estate?**

A. To ensure the agent gets the highest commission possible

B. To protect the interests of the agent's client above all else

C. To make sure the transaction closes as quickly as possible

D. To guarantee that the property sells for the highest price

Answer: B

The primary purpose of a fiduciary duty in real estate is to protect the interests of the agent's client above all else, ensuring that the client's needs and interests are the top priority in the transaction.

Day of the Exam

The day of the real estate license exam is a culmination of weeks, if not months, of preparation. It's the day when you'll put your knowledge and skills to the test, quite literally. This chapter aims to guide you through every aspect of the exam day, from the moment you wake up to the moment you submit your answers. We'll cover what to bring, what to expect, and how to manage your time and stress levels.

The Night Before

Final Review

The night before the exam is not the time for cramming. Instead, focus on a quick review of key concepts, formulas, and definitions. Make sure you have all the required documents and materials ready for the next day.

Sleep Well

A good night's sleep is crucial. Lack of sleep can affect your concentration and memory, so aim for at least 7-8 hours of quality sleep.

Morning of the Exam

Breakfast

Start your day with a balanced breakfast. Opt for foods that are high in protein and low in sugar to maintain energy levels.

Dress Comfortably

Wear comfortable clothing. Many test centers have strict policies about what you can bring into the exam room, so pockets may be checked.

Leave Early

Plan to arrive at least 30 minutes before the exam starts. This will give you time to find parking, check-in, and get settled.

At the Test Center

Check-in Process

Upon arrival, you'll need to present identification and possibly have your photo taken. Make sure to bring any required documents, such as your admission ticket or confirmation email.

The Testing Room

Once you're in the testing room, listen carefully to the proctor's instructions. You'll likely be assigned a computer for a computer-based test or given a test booklet for a paper-based test.

During the Exam

Time Management

Most exams are timed, so it's crucial to manage your time wisely. A common strategy is to go through the entire test, answering questions you're certain about first, and then revisiting the more challenging ones.

Read Carefully

Read each question and all answer choices carefully. Misreading a question can lead to an incorrect answer, even if you know the material.

Elimination Technique

If you're unsure about a question, use the process of elimination to narrow down your choices.

Stay Calm

It's natural to feel nervous, but try to stay as calm as possible. Take deep breaths if you start to feel anxious.

After the Exam

Preliminary Results

Some testing centers provide preliminary results immediately after the exam. However, these are not your final scores.

Review

After the exam, try to jot down questions or concepts that were challenging. This will be useful if you need to retake the exam.

Conclusion

The day of the exam is a pivotal moment in your journey to becoming a licensed real estate agent. Proper preparation can make the difference between passing and failing. Remember, this exam is not just a test of your knowledge, but also your ability to apply that knowledge in a timed, stressful environment. Good luck!

After the Exam: Next Steps

Congratulations, you've just completed your real estate license exam! Whether you're confident about your performance or anxious about the results, the journey doesn't end here. This chapter aims to guide you through the steps that follow the exam, from understanding your results to kickstarting your career in real estate.

Understanding Your Results

Preliminary Results

Some testing centers provide preliminary results immediately after the exam. However, these are not your final scores and should be treated as an initial indication.

Official Results

Your official results are usually sent to you via mail or made available online within a few weeks. These results are crucial for the next steps in your career.

Failed Attempts

If you didn't pass, don't despair. Many successful agents didn't pass on their first try. Take this as an opportunity to identify your weak areas and improve.

Re-taking the Exam

Waiting Period

Most states have a waiting period before you can retake the exam. Use this time wisely to prepare.

Re-application

You'll need to reapply and pay the exam fee again. Make sure to check if your state requires additional paperwork for retaking the exam.

Study Strategy

Revise your study strategy based on your previous performance. Focus on the areas where you scored low.

Licensing Process

Application

Once you pass the exam, the next step is to apply for your real estate license. This usually involves submitting an application form, proof of passing the exam, and sometimes, background checks.

Fees

There will be licensing fees, and these vary by state. Make sure to budget for this.

Issuance

Once your application is approved, you'll receive your real estate license. This is your ticket to legally practicing real estate.

Starting Your Career

Choosing a Brokerage

Your first job will likely be as a real estate agent under a brokerage. Research different brokerages to find one that aligns with your career goals.

Training and Mentorship

Many brokerages offer training programs and mentorship to new agents. Take advantage of these resources.

Building Your Network

Networking is crucial in real estate. Start building your professional network as soon as possible.

Marketing Yourself

Personal Brand

Developing a personal brand can set you apart from other agents. Consider your unique selling points and how you can market them.

Online Presence

In today's digital age, an online presence is essential. Consider creating a professional website and engaging in social media.

Traditional Marketing

Don't underestimate the power of traditional marketing methods like flyers, business cards, and local advertisements.

Continuing Education

State Requirements

Many states require ongoing education for real estate agents. Make sure you're aware of these requirements and plan accordingly.

Skill Development

The real estate industry is ever-changing. Keep updating your skills through workshops, courses, and seminars.

Financial Planning

Commission Structure

Understand the commission structure in your brokerage. This will help you set realistic financial goals.

Taxes

As a real estate agent, you're likely considered a self-employed individual for tax purposes. Make sure to consult a tax advisor for your specific situation.

Conclusion

The period following your real estate exam is a critical phase that can set the trajectory for your career. From understanding your results to starting your career, each step is an opportunity to establish yourself in the real estate industry. This chapter aims to be a comprehensive guide to navigating this crucial period, ensuring that you're well-prepared for the exciting journey ahead.

Career Development

Congratulations on passing your real estate exam and obtaining your license! The journey, however, is far from over. This chapter aims to guide you through the various stages of career development in the real estate industry, providing you with the tools and knowledge to achieve long-term success.

The First Year: Building Foundations

Choosing the Right Brokerage

Your first year in real estate is crucial for setting the tone for your career. Start by choosing a brokerage that aligns with your career goals and offers mentorship and training programs.

Setting Goals

Set achievable yet challenging goals for your first year. Whether it's closing a certain number of deals or earning a specific amount, having goals will keep you focused.

Networking

Begin building your professional network immediately. Attend industry events, join real estate associations, and connect with other professionals on social media platforms like LinkedIn.

Skill Development

Sales Skills

Real estate is a sales-driven industry. Invest in sales training programs and read books on sales techniques to improve your skills.

Communication Skills

Effective communication is key in real estate. Whether it's negotiating a deal or explaining contract terms to a client, your ability to communicate clearly can make or break your career.

Technical Skills

Familiarize yourself with industry-specific software and tools. From CRM systems to property management software, being tech-savvy will give you an edge.

Specialization

Residential vs. Commercial

Decide whether you want to specialize in residential or commercial real estate. Each has its own set of challenges and rewards.

Niche Markets

Consider focusing on a niche market, such as luxury homes, rentals, or foreclosures. Specializing can help you become an expert in a specific area, making you more attractive to clients.

Marketing and Branding

Personal Brand

Develop a personal brand that sets you apart from other agents. This could be based on your expertise, customer service, or unique selling propositions.

Digital Marketing

In today's digital age, having an online presence is essential. Create a professional website, engage in social media marketing, and consider running online ad campaigns.

Traditional Marketing

Don't neglect traditional marketing methods. Flyers, billboards, and local sponsorships can still be effective ways to generate leads.

Continuing Education and Certifications

State Requirements

Keep up with your state's continuing education requirements to maintain your license.

Additional Certifications

Consider obtaining additional certifications, such as Certified Residential Specialist (CRS) or Certified Commercial Investment Member (CCIM), to further your career.

Financial Planning

Budgeting and Expenses

Real estate can be a feast-or-famine industry. Learn to budget wisely, taking into account both your income and expenses.

Retirement Planning

It's never too early to think about retirement. Consider setting up a retirement fund and consult with a financial advisor for long-term planning.

Work-Life Balance

Time Management

Learn to manage your time effectively. Use tools like calendars and to-do lists to keep track of your tasks.

Stress Management

The real estate industry can be stressful. Develop stress management techniques, such as meditation or exercise, to maintain a healthy work-life balance.

Conclusion

Career development in real estate is a continuous, evolving process that requires dedication, skill-building, and strategic planning. From your first year to your eventual specialization, each stage of your career offers new challenges and opportunities for growth. This chapter aims to serve as a comprehensive guide for your career development, ensuring that you are well-equipped to navigate the complexities of the real estate industry successfully.

Conclusion

Dear Reader,

As you turn the final pages of "Texas Real Estate License Exam: Best Test Prep Book to Help You Get Your License!", I hope you feel a sense of accomplishment and preparedness. You've journeyed through the labyrinthine corridors of Texas real estate laws, navigated the complexities of property valuation, and even tackled the ethical considerations that will soon become a part of your everyday professional life.

The Importance of Preparation

This book was designed to be your comprehensive guide, your steadfast companion in the quest to become a licensed real estate agent in Texas. We've covered everything from the basics of property ownership to the intricate details of contracts and legal considerations. The mock exams at the end of each chapter were meticulously crafted to simulate the experience of the actual Texas Real Estate License Exam, ensuring that you are as prepared as you can be.

The Road Ahead

Passing the exam is just the beginning. The real estate industry is ever-evolving, and to stay ahead, continuous learning is essential. The chapters on career development, ethics, and specialty areas were included to give you a head start on what comes after the exam. Whether you choose to specialize in residential or commercial real estate, whether you aim to be a sales agent or aspire to own your brokerage someday, the tools for your success have been laid out in these pages.

The Power of Community

Remember, real estate is not just about properties; it's about people. Networking doesn't end when you pass the exam; in fact, it's just the beginning. Join local real estate associations, attend seminars, and never stop meeting people. Your network is your net worth in this industry.

A Note of Gratitude

I want to take a moment to express my gratitude for choosing this book as your guide. It's a crowded field out there, and the fact that you've trusted this resource means the world to us. We've done our best to make this book as comprehensive, informative, and practical as possible. Your success is our success, and we wish you nothing but the best in your real estate career.

Final Words

As you close this book, you're not just ending a chapter in your educational journey; you're opening a new one in your professional life. The real estate industry is challenging, but it's also incredibly rewarding. With the knowledge you've gained from this book, you're not just prepared for an exam; you're prepared for a fulfilling and lucrative career.

Thank you for allowing us to be a part of your journey. Good luck on your exam, and even more so, good luck in the exciting world of Texas real estate.

Made in United States
Orlando, FL
06 September 2024